Nature's Best
REMEDIES

Nature's Best
REMEDIES

THE WORLD OF HEALTH AND HEALING ALL AROUND YOU

NATIONAL GEOGRAPHIC

WASHINGTON, D.C.

Essential ingredients like pepper (page 1), lavender (pages 2-3), and herbs have appeared in cuisines and medicinal remedies around the world for centuries.

CONTENTS

The luscious pomegranate has been cherished as food and medicine for at least four millennia.

GETTING BACK TO NATURE

Today many people are getting back to nature when it concerns their health. As a complement to modern medicine, many are turning to medicinal herbs and other natural remedies that have been relied on for centuries to prevent and treat different conditions.

Types of Natural Remedies

Herbal remedies are available in many forms:

Infusion: A tea preparation, in which plant parts and hot water are mixed for a short time

Decoction: A longer tea preparation, in which plant parts are simmered in hot water for a longer time

Syrup: Plant parts added to a sugar-water or honey-water mixture

Powder: Ground, dried plant parts

Tincture: Essential plant components dissolved in a water and alcohol solution

Ointment: Powdered or essential plant parts added to an oily substance such as olive oil or petroleum jelly

Poultice: Fresh or dried plant parts applied to the skin with moist heat

A Few Precautions

Before trying any new therapies, consult your health care professional. If buying capsules and tablets, read labels to confirm that the product contains a "standardized extract." Standardization assures consistent dosages. Avoid combining herbs on your own. And most of all, be open to the healing powers of nature's best remedies.

CHAPTER ONE

THINKING CLEARLY

THE BRAIN AND THE NERVOUS SYSTEM

The comforting feeling of being centered is only possible with a balanced nervous system. A system that is disrupted can have attentions that wander, moods that plummet, and a peace of mind that can be lost. Fortunately, medicinal herbs are a time-tested, and in some cases scientifically supported, method to support a healthy mind.

The human body's communication network—the nervous system—is an incredibly vast, complex system that includes the brain, the spinal cord, and threadlike nerves that reach deep into every part of the body. Neurotransmitters (such as serotonin, dopamine, and norepinephrine) and hormones (such as cortisol, estrogen, and testosterone) exert powerful influences on mood, thought, appetite, and sleep. People often experience anxiety, anger, panic, insomnia, and mood swings when neurotransmitters or hormones exert a negative influence on the body and mind. The widely prescribed and commonly available remedies found in this chapter are effective, natural ways to lift the spirits and restore balance to the body's information superhighway.

Opposite: Butterflies perch on St. John's wort (*Hypericum perforatum*).
Above: Passionflower (*Passiflora incarnata*)

Asian Ginseng

THE CURE-ALL KING

Ginseng has been called the king of herbs, the root of heaven, and a wonder of the world. The most famous members in the ginseng family include about a dozen species in the genus *Panax,* which includes both American and Asian ginseng. This root has long been used in different cultures as a medicinal tonic to boost immunity, build strength, and improve overall health. In fact, the genus name is derived from the Greek *panakos,* meaning "cure-all."

One of the Asian species *(Panax ginseng)* has been shown to strengthen the nervous system in people suffering from injury and disease, prolonged emotional stress, physical exertion, and fatigue. Studies report that people taking Asian ginseng often feel more alert and show improvements in thinking, learning, concentration, and memory. Although it's mainly American ginseng *(Panax quinquefolius)* that has been clinically researched for use in diabetes, certain processed types of Asian ginseng, especially Korean red ginseng (steamed roots), may also help control diabetes, reduce cholesterol, promote mental clarity, and protect against certain types of cancer.

Dried ginseng roots are used in many natural cures.

▶ HISTORY

Ginseng has been a mainstay of medicine in China, Korea, and India for several thousand years. Ancient Indian texts speak of ginseng as a life-giving plant with magical powers. In the Far East, ginseng was thought to revitalize the entire body and all its systems. Asian ginseng was viewed not so much as a medicine but as a substance that strengthens the body's overall natural defenses to cure illness and protect against it. In modern herbal medicine such an herb or substance is called an adaptogen.

▶ USING GINSENG

Look for supplements made from pharmacopoeial-quality ginseng. Now extremely rare in the wild, the entire world's supply is cultivated, mostly in northeast China and South Korea. Supplements can be purchased in a variety of places, from your local grocery store to natural wellness centers. Check the labels of any product carefully to determine how much *Panax ginseng* is included in the formulation.

Extract: Standardized extracts of Asian ginseng containing 4 to 7 percent ginsenosides (active ingredients) are dosed 100 to 200 mg daily.

Tincture: Take 1 to 2 ml, up to 3 times daily.

Tea: Simmer 3 to 6 teaspoons of the root for 45 minutes in 3 to 4 cups water. Strain, cool, and drink a cup 1 to 3 times daily.

Capsules: Take 500 to 1,000 mg dried powdered root, 1 to 2 times daily.

▶ PRECAUTIONS

Blood pressure should be monitored when taking ginseng. Caution is advised for diabetics because ginseng can lower blood sugar levels. Asian ginseng can act as a stimulant, causing insomnia or

HOW TO HARVEST

Because wild populations were exhausted centuries ago, most Asian ginseng in the herbal marketplace is cultivated; China and South Korea are currently the world's largest producers. Cultivation requires considerable skill and training. Plants like rich, moist, well-drained, friable soils, high in humus and needing at least 80 percent shade, taking between 4 and 6 years to reach maturity. In autumn, roots are carefully dug, gently washed, and dried (for white ginseng) or steamed and dried (for red ginseng). Workers typically arrange harvested ginseng roots in neat rows on drying racks laid out in the sun. After drying, the roots are sorted, stored, or shipped.

anxiety; some people experience mild stomach upset or headache. Check with your physician to make sure that Asian ginseng will not interfere with any medications currently being taken. Using *Panax ginseng* for more than three months in a row is not advised; some researchers believe there are negative hormone-like side effects with prolonged use.

Common Name	Scientific Name	Parts Used	Therapeutic Uses
Asian ginseng	*Panax ginseng*	Roots	Memory booster, health tonic

Bacopa

SOOTHE AND IMPROVE YOUR MIND

Bacopa has been used for at least 3,000 years in Indian Ayurvedic medicine. Practitioners recommend it as a memory aid and nerve tonic. This plant has captured the interest of Western medical researchers, whose studies have shown that bacopa appears to help people process information faster and retain more knowledge. Herbal practitioners are further intrigued by the herb's use for promoting emotional well-being, physical endurance, and a healthy immune system.

▶ OBTAINING AND USING

Most of the world's bacopa is wild-harvested in India. An extract is made from the whole plant and then sold to botanical markets throughout the world.

Capsules: Generally, take 5 to 10 g powdered bacopa daily.

Tea: Generally, steep 1 to 2 teaspoons bacopa leaves in 1 cup water for 5 to 10 minutes, taken up to 3 times daily.

Tincture: Generally, take 1 to 2 teaspoons tincture a day, or 2 tablespoons syrup daily, or follow manufacturer's directions.

Often considered a weed, bacopa thrives in wet environments.

Extract: Standardized extracts contain 20 to 55 percent bacosides (effective ingredients); dosage is 150 mg twice daily.

▶ PRECAUTIONS

Bacopa may cause dry mouth, nausea, and fatigue, but appears to be relatively free of adverse effects in most studies. It may increase drowsiness when used in combination with sedative medications, and it may interact with thyroid medications. Nausea, bloating, or diarrhea may occur if taken on an empty stomach.

Common Name	Scientific Name	Parts Used	Therapeutic Uses
Bacopa	*Bacopa monnieri*	Aboveground parts	Cognition, memory, anxiety

Feverfew

NATURE'S MIGRAINE-PREVENTING POWERHOUSE

Used for over 2,000 years, feverfew helps reduce the frequency and severity of debilitating headaches called migraines. One of the more than 40 compounds in the leaf is parthenolide, shown to ease smooth muscle spasms and prevent the constriction of blood vessels in the brain, one of the leading causes of migraines.

Studies showing benefits from feverfew used a freeze-dried formulation of 50 to 100 mg daily, typically standardized as 0.2 to 0.35 percent parthenolide content. In some countries such as Canada, parthenolide consistency is required for feverfew products. Sometimes feverfew is blended with riboflavin (vitamin B_2) and magnesium, as these have also been shown to reduce migraine frequency.

Feverfew's dainty flowers prevent and relieve headache pain.

▶ OBTAINING AND USING

Feverfew is an easy-to-grow perennial, which provides a profusion of flowers year after year with only minimal attention. Commercially, feverfew products are sold in most health food stores.

Fresh leaf: Two leaves chewed daily to ward off migraines is the traditional treatment. **Warning:** The fresh leaf can cause mouth ulcers.

Capsules: Dosage is 50 to 250 mg daily. Check manufacturer's instructions. Do not exceed 4 mg of Parthenolide. Take with food or after eating.

▶ PRECAUTIONS

Clinical trials have shown feverfew to be safe and well tolerated. Anyone experiencing mouth ulcers from chewing the leaves should discontinue use. Pregnant women should not use feverfew.

GOOD TO KNOW

- **1525** *Banckes's Herbal* advocates feverfew for stomach disorders, toothaches, and bites.
- **1787** *Culpeper's Herbal* recommends feverfew for "pains in the head."
- **1791** *The Edinburgh New Dispensatory* suggests feverfew for hysteria and flatulence.
- **1973** A Welsh woman experiments with feverfew to relieve migraines and finds relief.

Common Name	Scientific Name	Parts Used	Therapeutic Use
Feverfew	*Tanacetum parthenium*	Leaves, flowering tops	Migraine headaches

Hops

A NATURAL GOOD NIGHT'S SLEEP

Hops flower clusters are called strobiles.

Best known as an ingredient in beer, hops can help bring on a good night's sleep. Studies have shown that hops, often in combination with valerian (another popular herbal remedy), can shorten the time it takes to fall asleep and help improve sleep quality. Placed under a pillow, a sachet of dried hops is considered an effective tool for inducing sleep.

▶ HISTORY

Hops was used medicinally by Native Americans to treat pain and insomnia. The Delaware applied small bags of heated hops leaves to aching teeth or ears. They also drank hops tea, as did the Cherokee, Mohegan, and Fox, to hasten sleep. In Europe, hops was used to ease pain in rheumatic joints; cure fevers; and treat heart conditions, diarrhea, and hysteria.

▶ OBTAINING AND USING

Hops is sold commercially in dried form as well as in capsules and extracts.

Tea: Steep 1 teaspoon hops strobiles (female flowers) in 1 cup water for 5 to 7 minutes. Add honey to taste. Drink 30 minutes before bed.

Capsules: Take 500 mg, 1 to 3 times daily; often taken in combination with valerian root.

Tincture: Take 2 ml, 1 to 3 times daily.

▶ PRECAUTIONS

Hops may have sedative effects, so don't drive or operate heavy machinery after taking. Hops may also stimulate increased hormonal activity in women, so those with a history of breast cancer or who are at risk for it should avoid hops until more is known. Safety in pregnancy is not known.

Common Name	Scientific Name	Parts Used	Therapeutic Uses
Hops	*Humulus lupulus*	Female flowers	Insomnia, anxiety

Kava

THE ROOT OF RELAXATION

Native to the South Pacific islands, kava root was traditionally brewed into a drink for royalty. Over time it was taken medicinally to relieve anxiety, combat fatigue, alleviate weakness, and treat chills and colds. In the 1770s, it was introduced to explorer Captain James Cook, who in turn introduced it to Europe.

Predominately used to relieve tension and anxiety, kava has been subjected to rigorous clinical trials, and its safety is still being investigated. Take precautions before using.

▶ OBTAINING AND USING

Purchase kava from a reputable manufacturer and use formulations that contain only the dried powdered

Kava roots have been used medicinally for centuries.

root. Trustworthy companies often include a statement that they do not use any stem or leaf. Look for products sold as "aqueous" extracts (meaning water is used as a solvent, not acetone or alcohol).

Tea: Simmer 1 to 2 teaspoons root in 1 cup water for 10 minutes. Strain. Drink 1 cup daily.

Extract: The dose used in clinical trials is 100 to 200 mg of root extract taken 3 times daily.

▶ PRECAUTIONS

Consult a health care professional if you have liver problems, use alcohol, or take acetaminophen or prescription medications. See a doctor if symptoms develop that may signal liver problems, such as fatigue, abdominal pain, vomiting, dark urine, pale stools, or yellow eyes or skin. Use is not recommended in pregnant or nursing women and those under 18.

Common Name	Scientific Name	Parts Used	Therapeutic Uses
Kava	*Piper methysticum*	Rhizomes, roots	Anxiety, menopause

Lemon Balm

SWEET-SMELLING STRESS RELIEVER

Lemon balm has been used to relieve stress and anxiety for millennia. In modern herbal medicine, it is combined with other calming herbs, such as valerian and hops, to reduce anxiety and promote sleep. Recent studies indicate that it may also improve secondary memory and the ability to learn, store, and retrieve information.

▶ HISTORY

Greeks and Romans drank wine infused with lemon balm—valued as a flavoring for food as well as a medicinal plant—for fevers and used the crushed leaves to treat wounds and bites. The Arabs praised it as a remedy for depression and for strengthening the memory. During the Middle Ages and Renaissance, lemon balm was used for easing anxiety and sleeplessness.

▶ OBTAINING AND USING

Lemon balm is a good addition to the herb garden. Harvested leaves can be dried quickly and easily. Available as dried herb, tea, tincture, and extract, lemon balm is safe and tolerated by all ages.

Tea: Pour 1 cup boiling water over 5 to 6 fresh leaves or 1 teaspoon dried leaf, and steep for 5 to 7 minutes. Strain. Add honey or stevia if desired. It's delicious with mint. Drink several times a day. **NOTE:** Do not give honey to children under 18 months of age, and substitute chamomile or spearmint for peppermint in children under 3.

Tinctures and extracts: Widely available. Use as directed.

Lemon balm leaves have a minty, calming fragrance.

Common Name	Scientific Name	Parts Used	Therapeutic Uses
Lemon balm	*Melissa officinalis*	Leaves	Anxiety, stress, digestion

Passionflower

A COLORFUL WAY TO RELAXATION

Passionflower is able to combat anxiety and sleep problems. Its exact mechanism is unknown but may involve inhibiting certain enzymes in the brain. Also, compounds in the herb bind to the same areas of the brain affected by a calming neurotransmitter called GABA, which helps explain why it is able to tone down the nervous system, leading to relaxation and sleep. Passionflower contains various flavonoids, compounds that are well-known antioxidants and may also contribute to antianxiety effects; flavonoids may be more concentrated in the leaves than other plant parts.

▶ OBTAINING AND USING

Passionflower is sold as a dried herb, capsules, and tinctures.

Infusion: Boil 1 to 2 teaspoons dried passionflower herb (excluding roots) in 2 cups water for 5 to 10 minutes. Strain and take 3 times daily and before bed for its calming and antianxiety effects.

Capsules and tablets: Take 1 to 2 350-mg capsules, 1 to 2 times daily; often combined with other herbs.

Tincture: Take 1 to 2 ml, 1 to 3 times daily; often combined with hops or with lemon balm.

▶ PRECAUTIONS

Some people experience drowsiness and dizziness with use of passionflower. It may increase effects of other sedative herbs or medications. It is generally not recommended during pregnancy. Passionflower also may increase the activity of or otherwise interact with blood-thinning medications.

RECIPE FOR HEALTH

STRESS-RELIEF TEA

Combine 1 cup dried chamomile, 1/4 cup lavender buds, 1/4 cup dried passionflower, 1/4 cup dried lemon verbena, 1/4 cup rose hips. (Dried herbs are available in bulk.) Add 1 tablespoon of mix per cup of tea in the teapot, plus 1 tablespoon for the pot. Pour boiling water in pot and steep for 5 minutes. Strain, sweeten, and enjoy!

Common Name	Scientific Name	Parts Used	Therapeutic Uses
Passionflower	*Passiflora incarnata*	Flowers, leaves, stems	Anxiety, insomnia

St. John's Wort

NATURE'S ANTIDEPRESSANT

Used for centuries to treat a variety of symptoms and ailments, St. John's wort wasn't incorporated into American medicine to treat nervous anxiety and depression until the late 17th century. In 2009, researchers evaluated 29 clinical trials and suggested that St. John's wort is more effective for mild to moderate depression than a placebo and as effective as standard prescription antidepressants with fewer adverse effects.

▸ OBTAINING AND USING

Commercial standardized extracts are made from the fresh or dried tops, calibrated to a defined chemical profile, depending upon manufacturer's specifications to ensure consistency.

Tea: Pour 1 cup boiling water over 1 teaspoon herb. Steep 5 to 10 minutes. Strain. Drink 1 to 3 times a day.

Tincture: Use 2 to 3 droppersful in 1 cup hot water or lemon balm tea.

Capsules and tablets: Most research has been done on products guaranteed to contain specific levels of key ingredients. To find a supplement, look for one standardized to 0.3 percent hypericin or 3 to 5 percent hyperforin. The dose for these products is 900 to 1,500 mg a day.

▸ PRECAUTIONS

St. John's wort appears to be safe, but individuals taking prescription medications should consult a doctor because of potential herb-drug interactions. Safety in pregnancy has not been established.

The sunny yellow flowers of St. John's wort

Common Name	Scientific Name	Parts Used	Therapeutic Use
St. John's wort	*Hypericum perforatum*	Dried flower tops	Minor depression

Skullcap

A SOOTHING SOURCE

A remedy for anxiety, skullcap is a native of North America.

Skullcap is used to soothe anxiety and sleep disorders. Modern herbalists suggest skullcap, thought to bind to a receptor of a neurotransmitter in the brain responsible for modulating anxiety, as a mild relaxant for treating nervous tension, anxiety, insomnia, and muscular tension.

▶ OBTAINING AND USING

Most of the commercial supply of *Scutellaria lateriflora* is wild-harvested, though there is limited cultivation in the Pacific Northwest.

Capsules: Take 850-mg capsules (containing leaves, stems, and fruits) twice a day, or 850- to 1,275-mg capsules (just leaves) 3 times daily, or follow manufacturer's directions.

Tincture: Some herbal experts recommend alcohol tinctures of the fresh plant to capture more of the healing compounds lost in drying the plant. Dosages range from 1 to 4 ml, taken 1 to 3 times throughout the day.

Tea: Steep 1 tablespoon dried leaves (with or without stems, flowers, or fruits) in a cup of hot water. Strain, cool, and drink 1 to 3 times a day.

▶ PRECAUTIONS

Though cases of severe liver toxicity have been reported, experts agree that they were caused by adulteration of skullcap products with a similar appearing but dangerous plant, germander. Drowsiness may result from skullcap; caution is advised for those taking pharmaceuticals for sleep or anxiety.

Common Name	Scientific Name	Parts Used	Therapeutic Uses
Skullcap	*Scutellaria lateriflora*	Leaves, stems, flowers	Anxiety, insomnia

Valerian

NATURE'S ANTI-INSOMNIA ALLY

Valerian has gone through numerous clinical trials to study the effect it has on people with insomnia. Results have been mixed, but it appears that if valerian does improve sleep, it must be taken for at least two weeks to achieve a benefit. Herbalists and naturopathic doctors suggest valerian as a safe alternative to commonly prescribed medications for insomnia and other sleep problems.

A traditional sleep remedy, valerian's roots have a pungent smell.

▶ HISTORY

Valeriana officinalis and other species of the herb were used in both traditional Chinese and Indian Ayurvedic medicine. The ancient Greeks used it to treat a variety of ills, and during the Middle Ages, valerian became something of a cure-all in Europe.

GOOD TO KNOW

Second century A.D.	Roman physician Galen recommends valerian for insomnia.
11th century	*Valeriana* is mentioned in an Anglo-Saxon leechbook, a book of medicinal recipes.
1942	Writer Agatha Christie includes valerian as evidence in *Five Little Pigs*.
1950	Valerian is dropped from the National Formulary of the United States.

▶ OBTAINING AND USING

Today valerian is widely available. The American Herbal Products Association gives valerian a class 1 safety rating, indicating that it is a very safe herb, but valerian could increase the effects of some drugs. Those taking antidepressants, antianxiety medication, or sleep aids should consult a knowledgeable practitioner before using it.

Tea: Steep 1 teaspoon dried valerian root in 1 cup water for 10 minutes. Strain. Drink 30 to 60 minutes before bed.

Capsules: Take 2 to 3 g dried valerian root 30 to 60 minutes before bed.

Extract: Doses of 300 to 900 mg valerian extract standardized to valerenic acid were used in clinical trials.

Tincture: Generally, take 5 to 10 ml 30 to 60 minutes before bed.

Common Name	Scientific Name	Parts Used	Therapeutic Uses
Valerian	*Valeriana officinalis*	Roots, rhizomes	Insomnia, anxiety

DO IT YOURSELF
Healing Gardens

Growing your own medicinal plants doesn't take a lot of space or a lot of time. You can grow from seeds, or purchase plants from a local nursery or farmer's market. These four plants will get you started:

Calming Chamomile. This herb (see page 58) can be grown easily from seeds in a sunny spot with sandy, well-drained soil. Two popular kinds—*Chamaemelum nobile* and *Matricaria recutita*—are actually different species but have the same medicinal effects.

Lovely Lavender. Buying seedlings from a nursery is the easiest way to grow lavender (see page 91). This drought-resistant plant thrives in the sun and well-drained soil.

Easy Echinacea. Echinacea (see page 24) can easily be grown from seeds. Plant in a sunny, well-drained spot in early spring when the soil is soft.

Stinging Nettle. Stinging nettles (see page 108) can take over a garden, so plant in containers or in an isolated area. The plants like shady, wet soil.

HARVEST AND STORE

The leaves and flowers of these plants can be dried and preserved. Gather the blossoms or leaves into a bunch and secure them with twine or a rubber band. Hang in a dark, well-ventilated space until fully dry. Keep the plants whole—do not crush the flowers or leaves. Keep the herbs in an airtight container labeled with the contents and date of harvest. If stored in a cool dry place, they should keep for a year.

CHAPTER TWO

BREATHING EASY

THE RESPIRATORY SYSTEM

Like many of the body's systems, the respiratory system goes about its job somewhat outside our conscious awareness, at least most of the time. We hardly notice the 22,000 breaths taken on average each day. With help from the diaphragm, the lungs form the core of the respiratory system, drawing in air, and in so doing, supplying the body with oxygen. From the lungs, oxygen enters the bloodstream and is rushed to organs, tissues, and cells, where it is exchanged for carbon dioxide that is taken back to the lungs and exhaled.

Despite its strengths, however, the respiratory system's constant exposure to the outside world leaves it vulnerable to bacterial and viral infections—such as the common cold, influenza, and tuberculosis. Yet as long as there have been respiratory illnesses, people have used medicinal herbs to combat them, and with much success. This chapter highlights remedies commonly recommended to treat respiratory system complaints.

Herbs like sage (above) and echinacea (opposite) have a long history of natural healing.

Echinacea

CUTTING SHORT YOUR STUBBORN COLD

Echinacea is a robust wildflower with a wealth of health benefits. One of the most well-studied herbs, it has gained a reputation for decreasing the severity and length of the common cold. It has been shown to have numerous effects on the immune system—from increased antibody responses to elevated interferon levels for fighting viruses to stimulation of white blood cells to work harder to fight infection.

There are several chemical compounds in echinacea that vary among the three species of the plant, plant parts, and extraction techniques: Polysaccharides, glycoproteins, and alkylamides all have medicinal effects that boost the immune system and inhibit viruses and bacteria. How echinacea works continues to be investigated. Daily use of echinacea does not seem to protect against getting a cold; however, some studies point to an effect of shortening a cold's length by a day or two. To see benefits, take adequate doses of good product at the first sign of illness.

▶ HISTORY

Echinacea's flowers consist of prickly, domed centers

Every part of the echinacea plant—from flowers to roots—is used in herbal medicine.

encircled by a single layer of lavender-hued petals. Native Americans were using at least three species of the plant medicinally. The herb was something of a universal remedy to Indians of the Great Plains and neighboring regions. The Omaha-Ponca chewed fresh echinacea root to dull toothache pain. Bathing the skin with the juice of echinacea roots helped heal burns and wounds. The Cheyenne used a tea brewed from powdered echinacea leaves and roots, or chewed the roots to soothe sore gums, mouth, and throat. Other tribes used various echinacea preparations to treat colds, coughs, colic, and even snakebites.

▶ OBTAINING AND USING

Today, echinacea roots and flowers are used. The entire world's supply of *Echinacea purpurea* is cultivated. It is sold in many forms in pharmacies, health food stores, and grocery stores.

Tea: Steep 1 to 2 teaspoons echinacea leaf/flower in 1 cup boiling water, or boil 1 teaspoon root in 1 to 2 cups water for 10 minutes.

Tincture: When coming down with a cold, take either a tincture of echinacea root or the expressed juice from the aboveground parts of fresh *E. purpurea* stabilized in alcohol. Every 2 hours, take 1 to 2 ml directly or diluted in water.

Capsules: The dose varies with each echinacea product, depending on the plant part used and the species.

▶ PRECAUTIONS

Anyone with an autoimmune condition must exercise caution in taking an immune-boosting herb like echinacea. Echinacea may inhibit certain liver enzymes, theoretically increasing blood levels of

HOW TO HARVEST

The entire world's supply of *E. purpurea* is cultivated. It is grown commercially throughout Europe, as well as in North America. *E. purpurea* is harvested for the herbal market when flowers are fully open, ensuring that key chemical constituents are at their peak. Harvest echinacea roots in late fall during the third or fourth year of a plant's life. Dry the roots before any processing or extraction of the herb's active compounds.

To keep wild-harvested stocks healthy, the plants must be carefully harvested by hand. Leave portions of rootstock in the ground to ensure regrowth.

medications such as itraconazole (for fungal infections), lovastatin (for lowering cholesterol), and fexofenadine (for allergies), so it is important to be careful when taking echinacea with these and other medications, including birth control pills. A rare allergic reaction can occur in people who are allergic to other plants in the Asteraceae (daisy) family. Some people experience very mild stomach upset or dizziness. High doses of echinacea can cause nausea.

Common Name	Scientific Names	Parts Used	Therapeutic Uses
Echinacea, coneflower	*Echinacea purpurea, E. angustifolia, E. pallida*	Whole plant	Colds and flus, wounds

Astragalus

NATURE'S PREVENTATIVE POWERHOUSE

Some natural remedies are best used at the first signs of illness, but astragalus works best as a preventive. Laboratory studies support this: Extracts of astragalus root improve the function of white blood cells, even increasing antibody levels in healthy people. Astragalus may also increase levels of interferons, immune-activating proteins that fight viral infections and tumors. These benefits help prevent upper respiratory infections, especially in those prone to colds and flus.

ASTRAGALUS "BUTTER"

In a double boiler, gently warm 1 cup tahini and 7 tablespoons pumpkin seed butter (available at health food stores). Stir in 3 tablespoons powdered astragalus root. Add 3 tablespoons sesame oil and stir to smooth consistency. (If too stiff, add up to 1 tablespoon sesame oil.) This nut butter substitute will keep 2 weeks in the fridge.

▶ OBTAINING AND USING

Astragalus is sold as dried roots, ground roots in capsule and tablet, as a liquid extract, or as an ingredient in herbal teas.

Tea: The daily dose of astragalus varies greatly; a typical dose is 3 to 6 tablespoons dried chopped root, simmered in 2 to 4 cups water for 10 to 15 minutes.

Capsules: Generally, dosage is 1 to 3 g dried, powdered root daily, depending on manufacturer's processing methods and medical condition being treated.

Tincture: Take 2 to 4 ml, 3 times a day.

▶ PRECAUTIONS

Astragalus is generally safe and very well tolerated. Anyone suffering an acute infection should not use, particularly in large amounts. Those with autoimmune diseases should consult with a health care provider before using any herbal medicine that could have immune-boosting effects.

Dried astragalus root has been used for centuries in Chinese medicine.

Common Name	Scientific Name	Parts Used	Therapeutic Uses
Astragalus	*Astragalus membranaceus*	Roots	Immune support, viral infection, tonic

Butterbur

ALL-AROUND ALLERGY STOPPER

Butterbur is capable of relieving the symptoms of seasonal allergies, such as itchy eyes, runny nose, and sneezing, without the drowsiness and other side effects associated with taking antihistamines. The roots of this plant reduce inflammation and appear to inhibit mast cells—a type of cell involved in nasal congestion and allergies. And today, as in the past, butterbur is still taken to relieve joint pain, to soothe coughs and bronchitis, and to ease irritations of the small intestine.

▶ HISTORY

Butterbur was used by the ancient Greeks to treat asthma. In medieval Europe, infusions of butterbur roots or leaves were a remedy for treating coughs, hoarseness, bronchial infections, and urinary tract complaints and to expel intestinal worms. It was given to lower fever and calm intestinal ailments.

▶ OBTAINING AND USING

Native to the Northern Hemisphere, the vast

Butterbur plants have enormous heart-shaped leaves.

majority of the world's supply is wild-harvested in eastern Europe and sold as herbal supplements.

Extract: A consistent amount of the main active compounds is desirable. Look for products that guarantee a minimum of 7.5 mg of petasin and isopetasin. For seasonal allergies, the dose for adults is typically 50 to 75 mg of the extract taken twice a day. The dose used in the studies for children ages 10 to 12 was 25 mg twice daily.

PRECAUTIONS

Butterbur naturally contains pyrrolizidine alkaloids (PA), a group of compounds that can be toxic to the liver. Only products labeled "PA free" should be used. Use of butterbur during pregnancy and lactation is discouraged.

Common Name	Scientific Name	Parts Used	Therapeutic Uses
Butterbur	*Petasites hybridus*	Leaves, rhizomes	Seasonal allergies, migraine headaches

Elder

A VERY BERRY COLD BUSTER

Ripe elderberries are loaded with vitamin C and antioxidants. Studies have found that elderberry syrup can help decrease the duration of cold and flu symptoms. Elderberry preparations can also reduce swelling in mucous membranes—and so relieve nasal and sinus congestion—and lessen sneezing, itchiness, and other symptoms of allergies.

▶ OBTAINING AND USING

European elder is found throughout most of Europe except in the extreme north, growing in habitats

Elderberries are rich in vitamin C and antioxidants.

similar to its North American counterpart, the common elder. Elders are easy to grow and can be bought at a nursery. Both the flowers and the fruits are used.

Elder flowers are harvested when in full bloom, simply by shaking the flower heads into a bag or basket. Once ripe in August or early September, the fruits are easily harvested.

Syrup: Sambucol is an elderberry syrup on the market that has been the subject of several research trials. The syrup contains 38 percent of an extract made from elder fruits. Recommended dosage is 2 teaspoons 4 times daily, although clinical trials have used up to 1 tablespoon 4 times daily for flu treatment.

Lozenge: Elder is combined with zinc, and often with other herbs, in a lozenge form. The lozenges may be used numerous times daily at the onset of a cold.

Common Name	Scientific Name	Parts Used	Therapeutic Uses
Elder	*Sambucus nigra*	Flowers, fruits	Colds, flus

Eucalyptus
REAL RESPIRATORY RELIEF

Eucalyptus's medicinal properties are found in its leaves.

Oil from eucalyptus leaves and flowers helps relieve upper respiratory infections, colds, coughs, and asthma. The volatile (or essential) oils, which contain 1,8-cineole (also called eucalyptol), help to relieve coughs by stimulating removal of mucus from the lungs, dilating airways, and fighting airway inflammation. Eucalyptus is an ingredient in many over-the-counter cough and cold remedies, including cough drops, chest rubs, and vapor baths.

▶ OBTAINING AND USING

Medicinally, *Eucalyptus globulus* is sold as dried leaves, capsules, teas, and essential oils. Essential oils, also an insect deterrent, make the leaves strongly aromatic.

Capsules: Eucalyptol capsules should be taken under medical supervision.

Tea: Steep approximately 1/2 teaspoon dried or fresh eucalyptus leaf in 1 to 2 cups water for 5 minutes. Drink 3 times daily for a cough.

▶ PRECAUTIONS

Ingested eucalyptus oil can cause nausea, vomiting, muscle weakness, breathing problems, increased heartbeat, and low blood pressure. These symptoms have been reported with ingestion of very small amounts—less than 1 teaspoon. Eucalyptus also may cause low blood sugar, so caution is urged for diabetics. Eucalyptus oil is a skin irritant and should always be diluted, especially for children. Never give children under two medications containing eucalyptus. Anyone taking prescription medications should check with a health care provider before beginning any eucalyptus treatment.

Common Name	Scientific Name	Parts Used	Therapeutic Uses
Eucalyptus	*Eucalyptus globulus*	Leaves, oil	Colds, cough, asthma, emphysema

Honey

STICKING IT TO COUGHS

Golden, sweet, and sticky, honey has been harvested by humans for millennia. A welcome addition to kitchens for its taste, humans have long known honey's medicinal qualities as well. Science has shown that honey has antibacterial properties and is effective at treating cuts, scrapes, and wounds. Honey is also used to treat cold and flu symptoms of coughs and sore throats. A 2007 study found that giving honey to children before bedtime provided better cough relief than dextromethorphan (DM), a cough suppressant found in many over-the-counter cold medications.

▶ OBTAINING AND USING

Honey is widely available for sale at grocery stores, health food stores, and farmers markets. More than 300 varieties are sold in the United States. Store honey in a cool, dark place.

A spoonful of honey is recommended to calm coughs.

Cough suppressant: Mix 1 tablespoon honey with 2 tablespoons freshly squeezed lemon juice. Heat gently until warm, and take 1 teaspoon every hour as needed.

Sore throat: Mix 2 teaspoons honey with 2 teaspoons apple cider vinegar in a cup of hot water. Sip frequently to ease sore throat pain.

▶ PRECAUTIONS

Honey is safe for adults. Never give honey to children less than a year old due to the risk of infant botulism, a form of food poisoning.

GOOD TO KNOW

- Almost all ancient Egyptian medicines contained honey, wine, and milk.
- The ancient Greeks drank oenomel, a beverage made of honey and unfermented grape juice.
- The Muslim prophet Muhammad recommended the use of honey for the treatment of diarrhea.
- In Ayurvedic medicine, honey is thought to keep the teeth and gums healthy.

Common Name	Scientific Name	Parts Used	Therapeutic Uses
Honeybees	*Apis*	Honey collected from honeycombs	Coughs, sore throats, laryngitis, wound care

Licorice

NATURE'S COUGH CALMER

Licorice root's demulcent, or tissue-coating, properties ease sore throats and soothe coughs, heartburn, and gastritis. Herbal practitioners prescribe licorice root for mouth ulcers, sore throat, laryngitis, coughs, and bronchial infections.

▶ OBTAINING AND USING

Licorice products are made from the dried root. Powdered, dried root preparations are made for teas, tablets, and capsules, as well as liquid extracts.

Lozenge: For a sore throat, a licorice lozenge used every few hours for several days allows the coating properties of licorice to soothe inflamed areas.

Tea: Add 1 to 2 teaspoons chopped licorice root to 2 cups boiling water. Boil for 10 minutes. Strain, cool, and drink a half cup 3 to 4 times a day for up to a week.

Tablet: Heartburn, gastritis, or related conditions requiring licorice treatment for more than a week respond well to deglycyrrhizinated licorice, or DGL, tablets (generally 1 to 2 380-mg tablets) before meals and at bedtime.

▶ PRECAUTIONS

Generally, licorice is safe if taken for less than a week at the doses listed above. Those with gastritis or heartburn should take a DGL product. Those with high blood pressure, kidney or heart troubles, or who are taking blood thinners or blood pressure medicines, should be cautious with any amount of licorice. Not recommended during pregnancy or lactation.

Dried licorice rhizomes

Common Name	Scientific Name	Parts Used	Therapeutic Uses
Licorice	*Glycyrrhiza glabra*	Rhizomes	Sore throat, cough, heartburn, gastritis

Marshmallow Root

MEDICINAL MULTITASKER

Marshmallow roots and flowers

Floating in hot cocoa or melting over a campfire, marshmallows are favorite confections. These sweet treats actually have their roots in a natural remedy made from the roots and leaves of the marshmallow plant. Marshmallow contains polysaccharides, a natural mucilage that soothes irritated mucous membranes from sore throats, coughs, and indigestion. It can also soothe dry, chapped skin when applied topically.

▶ OBTAINING AND USING

Marshmallow leaves and roots are the parts of the plant used for medicinal purposes. Dried leaves may be used in infusions, fluid extracts, and tinctures. Marshmallow roots are available dried, peeled, or unpeeled. Marshmallow is also sold as extracts, tinctures, capsules, and ointments.

Tea: Steep 1 teaspoon dried, chopped marshmallow root in 1 cup room-temperature water for 2 to 3 hours. Strain and drink 1/2 cup 2 to 3 times a day.

Infusion: Take 1 to 2 teaspoons to soothe an irritated throat or reduce cough symptoms.

▶ PRECAUTIONS

Marshmallow is generally considered to be safe. One study suggests that marshmallow may lower blood sugar levels; therefore, people with diabetes should talk to their health care provider before taking marshmallow.

Common Name	Scientific Name	Parts Used	Therapeutic Uses
Marshmallow root	*Althaea officinalis*	Leaves, roots	Sore throat, stomach upset

Mullein

SORE THROAT SOOTHER

Mullein's gray-green leaves and stems are used to ease symptoms of bronchitis, coughs, and other throat ailments by serving as both an expectorant and a coating, soothing herb for irritated respiratory tissues. Drinking mullein leaf or mullein flower tea soothes the throat and is a very old remedy for respiratory problems. It is thought that some respiratory benefits can be obtained by ingesting mullein as an infusion of the leaves or flowers. Various parts are used, including the leaves, flowers, and roots. Despite its long history of use for medicinal purposes, mullein has not been researched extensively, but it remains a respected remedy in herbal medicine today.

▶ OBTAINING AND USING

Mullein is not generally grown as a garden plant. It is sold in dried form, as well as in capsules and tinctures.

Delicate mullein flowers must be harvested by hand.

Tea: Pour 2 cups boiling water over 1 tablespoon dried mullein leaf and flowers. Strain. Drink 1 cup, 2 to 4 times daily.

Tincture: Take 1 to 4 ml, 3 times daily, or follow manufacturer's directions.

▶ PRECAUTIONS

Mullein seeds are toxic and should not be a part of any mullein extract, capsule, or tea. Aside from the seeds, mullein is considered to be safe and generally well tolerated.

RECIPE FOR HEALTH

MULLEIN COUGHING TEA

Combine 3 tablespoons fennel seed, 2 tablespoons dried mullein flowers, and 2 tablespoons dried peppermint leaf in a container with a tight-fitting lid. Place 1 tablespoon of this mixture in a cup, add just boiled water, and steep for 10 minutes. Sweeten with honey to enhance the expectorant properties, and sip slowly.

Common Name	Scientific Name	Parts Used	Therapeutic Uses
Mullein	*Verbascum thapsus*	Leaves, flowers	Ear infections, colds, bronchitis

Pelargonium

COMBATTING CHRONIC COUGHS

Pelargoniums have a strong tradition of medicinal use in Africa. *Pelargonium sidoides*—known in modern herbal medicine simply as pelargonium—has for centuries been a part of traditional Zulu, Xhosa, Basuto, and Mfengu healing. Herbal practitioners recommend the root to help reduce the symptoms of respiratory infections such as coughs, colds, sore throats, pneumonia, tonsillitis, and acute sinusitis, and to prevent secondary infections such as chronic bronchitis. It is often used as an alternative to antibiotics in some of these conditions.

GOOD TO KNOW

1920	Swiss tuberculosis patients are successfully treated with Stevens' Consumption Cure.
1983	German drug companies market *P. sidoides* root under the name Umckaloabo.
2002	Sales of Umckaloabo top $55 million annually.
2008	Zucol, a pelargonium-based cold remedy, is made available in the United States.

▶ OBTAINING AND USING

Pelargonium sidoides is sold as an extract, lozenges, and tinctures.

Extract: Umckaloabo is a clinically tested product that has been shown in clinical trials to be effective in the treatment of bronchitis and the common cold. The extract is available as an alcohol-based product and as an alcohol-free product as well. Follow dosing on the package.

Lozenges: Zucol lozenges contain pelargonium and are recommended for treating cold viruses.

Tincture: Alcohol-based tinctures of pelargonium are becoming increasingly available in the marketplace; dosage is generally 1 teaspoon (5 ml) taken 3 to 4 times a day.

Pelargonium's purple flowers and tuberous roots

▶ PRECAUTIONS

Pelargonium root extracts are generally well tolerated, though some users report mild stomach upset, rashes, and nervous system disorders. Safety in pregnancy and lactation has not been established.

Common Name	Scientific Name	Parts Used	Therapeutic Uses
Pelargonium	*Pelargonium sidoides*	Roots	Bronchitis, colds, flus, sinusitis

Sage

SAVORY AND SOOTHING

A classic seasoning herb for poultry and many savory dishes, sage is also an effective treatment for sore throats, coughs, and colds. Sage tea has long been used as a remedy, often as a gargle, and scientific studies have confirmed that this herb is highly effective for relieving sore throat. Sage exhibits antibacterial activity, which may explain its use for gastroenteritis, or for other minor gastrointestinal (GI) tract infections.

▶ OBTAINING AND USING

Sage can be grown at home from seeds or cuttings. Sage likes a loose, well-drained soil, without too much moisture. The majority of the world's sage supply is wild-harvested in the coastal mountains of Croatia, Montenegro, and Albania. Fresh and dried sage is available in most grocery stores; supplements and tinctures can be found in health food stores.

Sage leaves are used in both cooking and medicine.

Tea: Steep 1 teaspoon chopped sage in 1 cup water for 10 minutes. Strain. Drink or use as a gargle for sore throat.

Capsules: Take 500 mg sage leaf twice a day.

Tincture: Take 2 ml twice a day, or follow manufacturer's recommendation. A tincture of 5 ml can be added to 1 cup water and used as a gargle 3 times a day.

PRECAUTIONS

The amount of sage consumed as a culinary herb is safe, but do not exceed above recommended doses. Alcohol extracts of sage are not to be used internally for more than 1 to 2 weeks; a tincture diluted in water and used as a rinse or gargle is safe.

RECIPE FOR HEALTH

SAGE GARGLE

Combine 1 ounce dried sage leaves and 1 ounce dried thyme leaves in a coffee grinder. Grind and place in a quart mason jar. Cover with 16 ounces apple cider vinegar, stir, and close jar with tight-fitting lid. Let sit for 14 days, shaking periodically. Strain and put in a dark-colored bottle. This mouthwash can be safely used for sore throats and also to freshen breath.

Common Name	Scientific Name	Parts Used	Therapeutic Uses
Sage	*Salvia officinalis*	Leaves, flowers	Sore throat, coughs, colds, memory aid

Thyme

A COOKING AND HEALING HERB

Like sage, thyme is one of several fragrant herbs that doubles as a spice and a medicine. Thyme's aromatic compounds help to relieve coughs, probably in two different ways. Thyme is antispasmodic and an expectorant, meaning that the herb not only calms coughs but also helps clear bronchial mucus. It is also antibacterial and antiviral.

Several of the chemicals in the herb thyme, including thymol and carvacrol, account for its aroma, its expectorant effects, and for its inhibition of bacteria, viruses, and fungi. Today, herbal practitioners recommend thyme for coughs, colds, flu, bronchitis, and asthma. They also give the herb for digestive upsets, as thyme has a relaxing effect on the smooth muscles of the stomach and intestines.

▶ OBTAINING AND USING

Common thyme has been a staple

"pot herb" or "sweet herb" in gardens for centuries. Most thyme in commercial markets is cultivated in eastern and western Europe. Thyme extracts are available as capsules and syrups in a variety of doses and strengths. These products often combine thyme with other herbs thought useful for respiratory conditions. The specific use depends on the individual product.

▶ PRECAUTIONS

Thyme should be avoided in high doses or for long periods of time. As with any essential oil, thyme should be consumed only under the supervision of a medical professional.

> **RECIPE FOR HEALTH**
>
> **TEA THYME**
> Steep 1 teaspoon dried thyme leaf in a cup of hot water. Cover the cup with a saucer so that the important volatile oils do not evaporate. Strain and add honey to taste. Honey complements the expectorant action of thyme by coating the back of the throat. Drink a cup of the tea several times daily for coughs.

Thyme leaves are recommended for coughs and colds.

Common Name	Scientific Name	Parts Used	Therapeutic Uses
Thyme	*Thymus vulgaris*	Leaves, flowers, oil	Coughs, colds, flu

Plant essential oils are used in aromatherapy to restore health and balance to the body and mind.

DO IT YOURSELF
Aromatherapy

The use of aromatic essential oils for healing, known as aromatherapy, has ancient roots stretching back to Egypt and Persia. The idea underlying aromatherapy is that plant essential oils can be inhaled, or combined with a base and absorbed through the skin for health benefits. You can use these simple aromatherapy techniques at home:

Relaxing Room. In a spray bottle, combine 10 drops lavender essential oil with 1/2 cup water and 1 tablespoon vodka. Mix well. Mist a little of this mixture into the air.

Soothing Soak. While filling a tub with warm water, add 5 to 10 drops geranium oil. Close the bathroom door to hold the fragrance in the room and soak for about 15 minutes.

Lemon Lift Body Oil. Make your own invigorating body oil by adding 10 to 12 drops lemon essential oil to 2 tablespoons sweet almond oil. Store in a glass jar with a tight-fitting lid. Apply to damp skin after a shower or bath.

ESSENTIAL OIL SINUS STEAM BATH

Place 3 drops rosemary oil, 1 drop peppermint oil, and 1 drop eucalyptus oil in a large heat-safe bowl. Add 4 cups water, just off the boil. Sit in a chair and drape a towel over your head and shoulders. Lean over the bowl and inhale the scented steam. Keep breathing over the bowl of water, hovering at least 12 inches over the surface.

Precaution: People with asthma or reactive airways diseases, or who are allergic to any of the essential oils listed here, should not do this. It is also not appropriate for children under the age of three.

CHAPTER THREE

A HEALTHY BEAT

THE CIRCULATORY SYSTEM

The cardiovascular system is the body's transportation system, moving gases, hormones, nutrients, and disease-fighting cells around. There are three major components: the heart; the blood vessels; and blood, consisting of a fluid called plasma, red and white blood cells, and platelets.

Cardiovascular health is of the utmost importance. Poor diet and exercise, as well as stress and certain lifestyle choices, have been linked to many common cardiovascular problems—from high blood pressure (hypertension) and high blood cholesterol (hyperlipidemia or hypercholesterolemia) to diabetes and heart disease. An estimated 80 million American adults, or roughly one in three, have one or more forms of cardiovascular disease. The physicians of antiquity attempted to treat and prevent these problems using medicinal herbs. Modern herbalists still have some of these very old herbs, and some new additions, in their armory of plant prescriptions.

Opposite: The crimson fruits of the hibiscus plant are called calyxes.
Above: Cinnamon sticks (*Cinnamomum verum*)

Tea

A CIVILIZED CURE

Tea is second only to water as the world's most popular beverage. The three main varieties of tea—green, oolong, and black—come from the same plant, *Camellia sinensis,* but owe their differences to variations in processing the dried leaves.

Primarily, green tea has been used in traditional Chinese and Indian herbal medicine. It has long been valued as a stimulant, a diuretic, an astringent to control bleeding and help heal wounds, and a tonic for improving the condition of the heart and blood vessels. Traditionally, green tea was given to promote digestive health and to help regulate blood sugar.

Results from human, animal, and laboratory research suggest green tea may help prevent coronary heart disease; studies have shown a decrease in risk of stroke or heart attack in people who drink five or more cups of green tea daily. It aids in reducing cholesterol and may thwart diabetes by regulating blood sugar levels. Green tea also may reduce inflammation associated with inflam-

Black or green, tea begins with the leaves of *Camellia sinensis.*

matory bowel diseases, promote weight loss, and inhibit or even prevent the growth of many types of cancer.

▶ HISTORY

The tea plant has been cultivated in China for almost 5,000 years. According to legend, fabled Chinese emperor Shennong took the first sip of tea by chance in 2737 B.C. Tea drinking spread from China to Japan in the 12th century. The Dutch East India Company brought the first tea to Europe in the early 1600s. Tea drinking soon became firmly entrenched in England and its North American colonies, where struggles over tea's taxation and control of its trade helped ignite the American Revolution.

▶ OBTAINING AND USING

Tea is commercially cultivated in the subtropics and tropical mountains in East Asia. It is the most widely used beverage plant in the world. Tea is made from the young leaves and buds of the tea plant. Fermenting wilted leaves before final drying produces black tea. Green tea leaves are simply wilted before drying. Different processing methods produce tea with varying chemical profiles, and therefore flavors, as well as various medicinal attributes.

Infusion: Steep 1 teaspoon tea leaves in a cup of hot water (steeping time depends partly on desired strength). For weight loss, weight loss maintenance, and cancer and heart attack prevention, 4 to 6 cups daily may be necessary.

Decaffeinated products are an option and provide most medicinal benefits; however, caffeine and theophylline are part of how tea helps with weight loss. Adding milk to tea may decrease the absorption of polyphenols; the most medicinally effective

Tea plants are grown in rows upon rows on large plantations, and are commercially cultivated in the subtropics and tropical mountains in East Asia, where it has been grown on a large scale for many centuries. Harvesting tea leaves is a labor-intensive endeavor; a gentle touch is essential to avoid bruising the tender leaves. Only the youngest shoots are plucked, typically the last two or three leaves plus the bud on a branch. Then the leaves are dried and processed according to the type of tea desired.

cup of tea is made with just water, perhaps with a bit of sweetener to taste.

Capsules: Capsules of dried tea leaves standardized to polyphenol content are available; generally, dosage is 500 mg once or twice daily.

▶ PRECAUTIONS

There are few problems with tea, though some people feel restless and anxious as a result of the caffeine. Green tea extracts have been associated with a few reports of liver toxicity.

Common Name	Scientific Name	Parts Used	Therapeutic Uses
Tea	Camellia sinensis	Leaves, buds	Heart health, cholesterol, anti-inflammatory

Bilberry

A BLUE CLUE TO CARDIOVASCULAR HEALTH

Cousin of the blueberry, bilberry is a sweet, dark purple fruit loved by people and birds alike. Bilberry has a long history of use as both food and medicine. The fruit was enjoyed for its sweet-sour taste as well as for its abilities to treat digestive problems. This is likely due to the presence of tannins that have astringent and anti-inflammatory activity.

Bilberry fruit is rich in anthocyanosides, plant pigments that act as powerful antioxidants in the body. Researchers have found that these compounds may help prevent heart disease, oxidative stress, and inflammation. Bilberry has no known adverse effects, but should not replace appropriate medical care.

RECIPE FOR HEALTH

BILBERRY SYRUP
Combine 1-1/2 cups fresh or frozen bilberries (blueberries can be substituted), 1 tablespoon lemon juice, 2 tablespoons dark honey, and a pinch of ground cloves in a saucepan. (Add 2 tablespoons water if using fresh berries.) Bring to a boil over medium heat, reduce to low heat, and simmer 5 to 10 minutes until juices are slightly thickened. Refrigerate up to 10 days. Pour over pancakes or waffles.

▶ OBTAINING AND USING

Fresh bilberry fruits are available only for a limited two-week period, so the careful timing of harvest is important for commercial production. Teas and extracts are also commercially available.

Fresh berries: Eat 1 cup a day of fresh fruit. (American blueberries can be substituted if bilberries are not available.)

Tea: Simmer 1 tablespoon dried berries in 2 cups water for 20 minutes. Strain. Drink 1/2 cup every 3 to 4 hours for diarrhea.

Extracts: Dosage range is usually 360 to 600 mg a day of an extract standardized to contain 25 percent anthocyanosides (also written as anthocyanadins).

Ripe bilberry fruits

Common Name	Scientific Name	Parts Used	Therapeutic Uses
Bilberry	*Vaccinium myrtillus*	Fruits, leaves	Antioxidant, anti-inflammatory, indigestion

Cacao

HAPPY MOUTH, HEALTHY HEART

Cacao, a small tree native to Central and South American forests, produces large pods packed with dark brown seeds, from which come cocoa, chocolate, and cocoa butter.

Studies link chocolate consumption to improved cardiovascular health. Chocolate's main medicinal effects come from a group of antioxidant, anti-inflammatory compounds called polyphenols. Similar compounds are found in green tea, red wine, and many fruits and vegetables.

Eaten in moderation, pure dark chocolate has been shown to both lower blood pressure and help reduce LDL ("bad") cholesterol in the blood. Chocolate may reduce the risk of heart attack by slowing blood clotting in vessels. Recent research has also shown that eating chocolate may increase a person's chance of surviving a heart attack.

Dried cacao seeds, or beans, will be roasted and ground.

▶ OBTAINING AND USING

Cacao is produced in many tropical regions around the world to be exported for chocolate manufacture. Major producing regions include West Africa, Malaysia, and Brazil, with limited production in Mexico, Central America, and many Caribbean islands.

When purchasing for health purposes, choose a dark chocolate of at least 70 percent cacao to maximize the polyphenol content and medicinal benefits.

Eat in moderation: The fat content of chocolate carries a calorie-heavy punch, so eating too much can add up and counteract any health benefits you might receive.

GOOD TO KNOW

1500 to 400 B.C.	The Olmec are believed to be the first to cultivate cacao as a crop.
A.D. 600	The Maya established the earliest known cacao plantations in Mexico's Yucatán region.
1753	Swedish naturalist Carolus Linnaeus gives cacao the scientific name *Theobroma*.
1875	The first milk chocolate, made in Switzerland, appears in the international marketplace.

Common Name	Scientific Name	Parts Used	Therapeutic Uses
Cacao	*Theobroma cacao*	Seeds	Heart health, antioxidant

Cinnamon

A STABILIZING SPICE

Found in almost any kitchen, cinnamon probably deserves a spot in the medicine cabinet too. Cinnamon is recommended to improve peripheral circulation, thus increasing blood flow to the hands and feet. More recently, cinnamon has been shown to possibly have an insulin-like effect in the blood and may help stabilize blood sugar levels in people with type 2 (adult-onset) diabetes. It also may reduce blood cholesterol levels, but more research is needed on both these effects.

Strips of bark cut from cinnamon trees are rolled and dried to form cinnamon sticks.

PRECAUTIONS

Cinnamon is well tolerated, though the volatile oil can cause a skin rash. Cassia and other cinnamons contain small amounts of coumarin. To be safe, caution is advised for anyone with liver problems. Due to its blood-thinning effects, cinnamon in quantities greater than use as a spice should end at least one week prior to surgery. Medicinal doses are not recommended during pregnancy. Close monitoring of blood sugar levels in people with diabetes is warranted to avoid unsafe lowering of blood sugar.

▶ OBTAINING AND USING

The most commonly used varieties in herbal medicine are true cinnamon (*Cinnamomum verum*) and Chinese cinnamon (*C. cassia*), a close relative. Whole cassia and cinnamon bark and ground cassia and cinnamon are considered separate commodities, but by the time cinnamon reaches American consumers, it may be an admixture of several species and grades.

Powder: For diabetics, powdered cinnamon spice is an option—but for positive effects on blood sugar levels it is necessary to use approximately 1 teaspoon daily. The common spice purchased in grocery stores is not necessarily cassia cinnamon.

Capsules: Cinnamon capsules range in dose and suggested use; studies in type 1 and 2 diabetics used 1 to 6 g cinnamon a day, taken in divided doses.

Common Name	Scientific Name	Parts Used	Therapeutic Uses
Cinnamon	*Cinnamomum verum*	Bark	Diabetes, antioxidant

Garlic

CLOVES THAT CURE

Cloves of garlic

Garlic has a strong history in herbal medicine as well as cuisine. Garlic is used to prevent and treat heart disease, regulate cholesterol levels, reduce high blood pressure, and strengthen the immune system. It's also recommended for digestive complaints, as it may help inhibit gut bacteria, including *Helicobacter pylori,* implicated in ulcers and stomach cancer, and a number of diarrhea-causing organisms. Fresh garlic also impairs many organisms that cause colds. In fact, a preliminary study found that taking a garlic supplement may help prevent common colds.

▶ OBTAINING AND USING

Fresh and dried garlic are widely available, as are garlic supplements.

Eating: One of the easiest ways to take garlic is simply to eat it! Crush a couple cloves and put them in olive oil, add a dash of lemon, and toss over a salad.

Capsules: If buying garlic in capsule form, look for products standardized to allicin, a key ingredient. Research suggests garlic products providing 4 to 8 mg allicin daily are optimal.

▶ PRECAUTIONS

There is a small risk that eating larger quantities of raw garlic (more than 4 cloves a day) can affect platelets' ability to form a clot, so reduce consumption 10 days before surgery and do not exceed this amount if taking anticoagulant medications. Garlic can also interfere with medications used to treat HIV infection.

Common Name	Scientific Name	Parts Used	Therapeutic Uses
Garlic	*Allium sativum*	Bulb	Heart health, indigestion

Ginkgo

A PREHISTORIC PRESCRIPTION

Surviving for more than 200 million years, *Ginkgo biloba* leaves have been an herbal remedy for many centuries.

Ginkgo contains potent antioxidants called glycosides, which protect nerve cells, and terpene lactones, which reduce inflammation. Ginkgo is used for poor circulation and to reduce the pain of peripheral vascular disease. Studies do show that ginkgo improves arterial function.

Ginkgo leaves have a distinctive fan shape.

▶ OBTAINING AND USING

Ginkgo leaves are fan-shaped and bilobed, with prominent forked veins. Much of the world's ginkgo leaf supply comes from specialized farms in South Carolina, the Bordeaux region of France, and plantations in China.

Tea: Steep 1 teaspoon ginkgo leaf in 1 cup water for 5 to 7 minutes. Strain. Drink 1 to 2 cups daily.

RECIPE FOR HEALTH

A SPOT OF GINKGO TEA

Mix 1 ounce ginkgo leaves and 1 ounce green tea leaves together and store in a glass jar. To prepare tea: Pour 1 cup boiling water over 1 heaping teaspoon herbs. Steep 5 to 7 minutes. Strain. Add small amount of honey and/or lemon juice. Drink for a delightful afternoon tea.

Tincture: Generally, take 3 to 5 ml twice a day, or follow manufacturer's directions.

Extract: Most research has been conducted on doses of 120 mg taken twice a day of extracts standardized to 24 to 27 percent flavone glycosides and 6 to 7 percent triterpenes.

▶ PRECAUTIONS

Ginkgo leaf is considered safe, as shown in large clinical trials and wide use. But there may be effects on blood clotting. Those taking medications to prevent blood clots should consult a health care professional before using. Stop taking ginkgo at least three days before surgery. Use in pregnancy is not recommended due to risk of increased bleeding.

Common Name	Scientific Name	Parts Used	Therapeutic Uses
Ginkgo	*Ginkgo biloba*	Leaves, seeds	Circulation, mental health, antioxidant

Grapes and Grape Seed

CHEERS! TO HEART HEALTH

Health care professionals recommend standardized grape seed extract to lower high cholesterol and high blood pressure and treat a host of circulatory ailments, including coronary heart disease, chronic venous insufficiency, and varicose veins. Chemical compounds in red wine may also reduce the risk of developing heart disease.

A growing body of research is showing that extracts from grape seeds are beneficial for your health. Grape seeds contain powerful antioxidants known as proanthocyanidins, which science is finding may help prevent heart disease, diabetes, and cataracts. Human studies have found grape seed extract can lower blood pressure and cholesterol and reduce inflammation.

Grapes are the source of wine and grape seeds, rich in health-promoting substances.

GOOD TO KNOW

6000 B.C.	Wine made from grapes dates at least from this time.
Second century B.C.	Grape vines were introduced to China, and the first Chinese grape wine was produced.
A.D. 500	Grape growing and winemaking preserved the church after the fall of Rome.
1869	Thomas B. Welch introduced unfermented grape juice as a beverage.

▶ OBTAINING AND USING

Vitis vinifera is the source of the common grape from which grape juice, raisins, wine, and a by-product used in herbal preparations, grape seeds, are derived.

Wine: Women can take 1 serving a day, 1 to 2 for men. Do not consume during pregnancy.

Grape juice: Drink 4 to 6 ounces of dark purple grape juice a day.

Grape seed extract: Take 300 to 600 mg a day.

Common Name	Scientific Name	Parts Used	Therapeutic Uses
Common grape vine	*Vitis vinifera*	Seeds	Heart health, antioxidant

Hawthorn

A HEART'S BEST FRIEND

Hawthorn flowers, leaves, and fruits hold benefits for the heart.

Long cultivated as an ornamental shrub, hawthorn is today used for a variety of heart-related conditions. It can help improve heart function and relieve shortness of breath and fatigue in those suffering from congestive heart failure, and may also help relieve chest pain (angina) caused by restricted blood flow to the heart. Research shows that hawthorn improves blood flow through the heart, ensuring that muscle cells are well oxygenated. Herbal practitioners also recommend hawthorn for reducing high blood pressure, high cholesterol, and the buildup of fatty plaques in blood vessels, which can lead to atherosclerosis.

▶ OBTAINING AND USING

Hawthorn is available in capsules, tinctures, and standardized extracts, as well as dried leaves, flowers, and berries.

Tea: Steep 2 teaspoons hawthorn leaves and flowers in 12 ounces water for 10 minutes. Strain and drink 1 to 2 cups a day.

Tincture: Generally, take 5 ml twice daily.

Standardized extract: HeartCare is a product standardized to the same specification as the proprietary hawthorn product used in the large SPICE trial (of extract WS-1442).

▶ PRECAUTIONS

Hawthorn appears to be safe and well tolerated. Hawthorn is best used under the supervision of a medical professional, for anyone who suffers from congestive heart failure or is being treated for heart disease or hypertension. Hawthorn can take a few weeks to have an effect.

Common Name	Scientific Name	Parts Used	Therapeutic Uses
Hawthorn	*Crataegus laevigata*	Leaves, flowers, fruits	Heart health

Hibiscus

A TROPICAL CURE

Hibiscus sabdariffa goes by many names: hibiscus, roselle, Jamaican sorrel, Queensland jelly plant, sour-sour, and Florida cranberry. Widely cultivated in the tropics, hibiscus's exact origins are unclear. It was adopted in the New World when it was brought over by African slaves.

Hibiscus's role in cardiovascular health is an exciting area of research. Scientists have confirmed that constituents exhibit potent antioxidant activity and exert beneficial effects on blood pressure and cholesterol. Hibiscus appears to lower blood pressure in part because of its diuretic effect and also by

inhibiting angiotensin-converting enzyme (ACE), a compound that increases blood pressure.

▶ OBTAINING AND USING

Hibiscus is sold dried, as a tincture, and in capsules.

Tea: Pour 1 cup boiling water over 2 teaspoons chopped hibiscus. Steep for 15 minutes. Strain and add sugar or honey. Serve chilled or hot.

Tincture: Take 1 teaspoon twice daily.

Capsules: Take 1,000 mg dried hibiscus 2 to 3 times a day.

▶ PRECAUTIONS

There are no known adverse effects of hibiscus; however, those taking prescription diuretics should use sparingly. High blood pressure or heart disease patients should consult a health care provider before using natural remedies for treatment. Note that hibiscus is toxic to dogs.

Hibiscus calyxes have an astringent taste, similar to French sorrel.

Common Name	Scientific Name	Parts Used	Therapeutic Uses
Hibiscus	Hibiscus sabdariffa	Fruit (fleshy calyx)	Heart health, diuretic

Horse Chestnut

SEEDS OF HEALTHY CIRCULATION

In folk tradition, horse chestnut bark and fruit were used to prepare topical ointments that could be used to relieve hemorrhoids and swelling from sprains and strains. In Europe today, horse chestnut seed extract (HCSE) is widely used for treating many vascular conditions, as well as sports injuries. Interest in the extract's medicinal applications is growing in the United States. Herbal practitioners and physicians most commonly suggest HCSE for cases of chronic venous insufficiency (CVI), a condition characterized by leg swelling, varicose veins, leg pain, and skin ulcers.

Modern herbalists use extracts from the tree's seeds for therapeutic uses.

GOOD TO KNOW

- In England, horse chestnuts are called conkers.
- Horse chestnut trees were introduced to Europe from Asia in 1576.
- Raw horse chestnuts are poisonous to people.
- Deer, squirrels, and boars are among the few animals that can eat horse chestnuts.

▶ OBTAINING AND USING

Horse chestnuts are commercially grown in Poland and elsewhere in eastern Europe. Standardized extracts and topical creams are available in stores.

Standardized extract: Given the toxicity with unprocessed horse chestnut seeds, only appropriately prepared seed extracts should be used. Most studies used a daily dose of 600 mg a day of HCSE containing 100 to 150 mg of aescin.

Topical: Gel preparations of horse chestnut containing 2 percent aescin are commercially available. Use as directed.

▶ PRECAUTIONS

Properly prepared standardized extracts of horse chestnut seed appear to be safe and well tolerated. Unprocessed horse chestnuts should not be eaten or used as herbal medicine as they are associated with serious toxicity. Do not apply gel to broken or ulcerated skin.

Common Name	Scientific Name	Parts Used	Therapeutic Uses
Horse chestnut	*Aesculus hippocastanum*	Seeds, leaves, flowers, bark	Varicose veins, chronic venous insufficiency

DO IT YOURSELF
Container Gardens

Not having a backyard is no excuse not to have a garden. Small spaces can host medicinal gardens. These four plants are a veritable medicine cabinet, giving you the ability to treat a host of problems. Most do well when planted in potting mix in a well-drained pot.

Aloe. Aloe plants (see page 84) are well suited for indoor life. They like sun and well-drained soil. Water it when the soil is completely dry.

Lemon Balm. Hardy, strong, with a beautiful scent, lemon balm (see page 16) soothes anxiety and eases digestive troubles. Planted in a sunny spot and well watered, it flourishes.

Peppermint. Plant peppermint (see page 64) in a deep, well-draining container. Place the plant where it receives at least four hours of sun.

Thyme. Thyme (see page 36) comes in many varieties, but all grow best in full sun and well-drained soil. Harvest the leaves as you need them, whether for cooking or colds!

FIZZY LEMON BALM SODA

Use fresh lemon balm leaves from your container garden in this refreshing fizzy drink. In a heatproof bowl, add 2 cups fresh lemon balm leaves and 1 quart just boiled water. Stir to combine and steep 30 minutes. Strain and let the liquid cool. Add 2 tablespoons honey and stir well. Refrigerate until cold. When ready to serve, add 1 quart carbonated water to the lemon balm mixture and pour into ice-filled glasses. Garnish with a slice of fresh lemon and a sprig of fresh lemon balm.

CHAPTER FOUR

FUELING UP

THE DIGESTIVE SYSTEM

Eating is not just a pleasure, it's also a necessity. Food gives us energy after it's digested or broken down into small molecules of nutrients. The digestive system is made of several connecting parts: the mouth, esophagus, stomach, and intestines. Two adjunct organs, the liver and the pancreas, produce additional digestive juices that enter the small intestine via tiny ducts. When the digestive system runs smoothly, things are good. But when digestion goes awry, life can be most unpleasant.

Digestive complaints are caused by lots of issues: improper storage and handling, poor nutrition, infectious diseases, and stress. The herbalists of antiquity and today have found stomach-soothing plants whose actions are gentle, effective, and documented by scientific research. Medicinal plants have a great deal to offer when it comes to digestive troubles. Not only can many of these cures be treated as foods or flavorings to spice up dishes, but they can also help the body digest them.

Opposite: A cup of chamomile tea is one way to tame stomach troubles.
Above: Green cardamom pods (*Elettaria cardamomum*)

Ginger

SPICE UP YOUR LIFE

Ginger is native to Asia, where it has been used as a spice for at least 4,400 years. Over the centuries, it has become one of the world's most popular culinary flavorings. Its intensely clean and slightly sweet flavor, coupled with its zesty heat, is an essential element in everything from Indian curries and Thai stir-fries to gingerbread and ginger ale.

Ginger's genus name, *Zingiber*, is derived from the Greek *zingiberis*, which, in turn, came from the Sanskrit *sringabera*, meaning "horn shaped."

Medicinally, ginger is primarily used to treat digestive problems, but it has many other applications as well. Herbalists prescribe ginger root to prevent or treat nausea and vomiting caused by motion sickness. Unlike many prescription and over-the-counter motion sickness medicines, ginger does not cause drowsiness or dry mouth. Ginger also safely relieves nausea associated with pregnancy, cancer chemotherapy, and postoperative recovery, and has antiseptic properties that can relieve infections of the digestive tract and the effects of food

Ginger's roots contain a strong fragrance and compounds that aid digestion.

poisoning. Ginger tea is used to treat colds, flu, headaches, and painful menstruation. Ginger is also used in traditional medicine to reduce pain and inflammation associated with arthritis and ulcerative colitis.

▶ HISTORY

Since ancient times, ginger has played a role in Arabic, Indian, and Asian herbal medicine. It has been an essential ingredient in traditional Chinese medicine since the fourth century B.C. In ancient India, ginger was used to treat digestive upsets and intestinal gas, and to stimulate circulation in the body's extremities. It was known by the Sanskrit name *vishwabhesaj,* meaning "universal medicine." The Greeks and Romans imported ginger from the East and ate it as a cure for intestinal parasites. During the Middle Ages, it was held in such high esteem that it was said to have come from the Garden of Eden.

▶ OBTAINING AND USING

Ginger has been cultivated in tropical Asia since ancient times, but its origins are obscure. No wild forms of ginger are known in tropical Asia. Perhaps originating in India, it spread throughout the Asian tropics before recorded history. Fresh ginger, ground ginger, and ginger teas can be purchased at most grocery stores. Ginger extracts and capsules can be found at health food stores.

Fresh ginger tea: Slice 1 inch fresh ginger rhizome into small pieces. Simmer in 2 cups water on low heat for 15 minutes. Strain. Drink 1 to 3 cups a day for coughs and colds and to enhance circulation.

Dried ginger tea: Pour 1 cup boiling water over 1/4 to 1/2 teaspoon ginger powder and steep for 10 minutes. Pour liquid tea off and discard powder. Drink 1 cup after meals for gas/bloating or to ease nausea.

HOW TO HARVEST

Ginger is grown locally and commercially throughout the tropical regions of the world. The rhizomes (underground stems) are highly aromatic, with thick, branching lobes, varying in size and shape depending on the cultivated variety. Usually the rhizome's outer lobes—with a bud or an eye—propagate ginger. Ginger likes a moderately rich loam and warm, humid, sunny conditions. It is usually harvested about nine months after planting. Products include fresh rhizomes (green ginger), dried ginger, preserved ginger, and essential oils.

Capsules: Take 250 to 500 mg 2 to 3 times a day.

Extracts: Concentrated extracts are typically used for osteoarthritis. Use as directed.

▶ PRECAUTIONS

Adding ginger to the diet is safe for young and old, although ginger may possibly cause mild heartburn in some. Pregnant women should not take more than 1 g dried ginger a day. Do not combine high doses of ginger with anticoagulant drugs (blood thinners) without medical supervision.

Common Name	Scientific Name	Parts Used	Therapeutic Uses
Ginger	*Zingiber officinale*	Roots, rhizomes	Nausea and vomiting, inflammation

Barberry

DIGESTION WARRIOR

The genus *Berberis* contains hundreds of species of deciduous and evergreen shrubs, the best known of them being barberry. Native to central and southern Europe, northwest Africa, and western Asia, the plant now grows all over the world. Many countries cultivate it for its fruits—sharply acidic berries high in vitamin C, but barberries also have medicinal value.

Barberry root bark contains berberine, a powerful alkaloid that fights a plethora of infectious organisms, including those that cause diarrhea. Barberry inhibits the abilities of germs to reproduce and cuts down on the time of infection.

▶ OBTAINING AND USING

Berberine is available as a pharmaceutical drug in some countries and is sold as a supplement in the

GOOD TO KNOW

- A popular Russian candy is made with barberry fruits, which are pictured on the wrapper.
- In Europe, tart barberry fruits are often made into jam.
- Barberry plants can grow as high as 9 feet tall!
- Barberry roots and stems can be used to make yellow dye.

United States. Barberry capsules, fluid extracts, tinctures, and topical ointments are available, as are unprocessed dried roots.

Tea: Steep 2 to 4 g dried root in boiling water for 10 to 15 minutes. Drink 3 times daily.

Tincture: Take 30 to 60 drops, 1 to 3 times daily.

Dry extracts: Take 250 to 500 mg, 3 times daily.

▶ PRECAUTIONS

When taken properly, side effects are rare. Extremely high doses have been associated with cases of nosebleeds and vomiting. Barberry should not be taken for more than a week without consulting your health care provider. Pregnant and breast-feeding women should not use barberry or any products containing berberine.

Barberry root bark has effective antimicrobial agents.

Common Name	Scientific Name	Parts Used	Therapeutic Uses
Barberry	*Berberis vulgaris*	Stem, root bark	Digestive aid, diarrhea, heartburn

Cardamom

A SPICY SOLUTION

Originating in southern India, cardamom is the third most expensive spice in the world after saffron and vanilla. The spice is a central part of Indian as well as Scandinavian cuisine. Cardamom seeds are also used medicinally to treat digestive ailments including heartburn, intestinal spasms, irritable bowel syndrome (IBS), intestinal gas, constipation, liver and gallbladder complaints, and loss of appetite. It is also used to treat everything from the common cold, cough, and bronchitis to sore mouth and throat, and anything

with a tendency toward infection. Some people use cardamom as a stimulant and for urinary problems.

▶ OBTAINING AND USING

Guatemala is the world's largest supplier of commercial cardamom. The green and black varieties are the most widely available. At the grocery store, you can find them in pods or ground. Essential oils and capsules are available at health food stores.

Seeds: Take about 1.5 g ground seeds a day.

Tea: Crush 1 teaspoon cardamom seeds. Steep these in 1 cup boiled water for 10 minutes before drinking.

▶ PRECAUTIONS

Cardamom is safe for most people with few known side effects. Pregnant and breast-feeding women do not need to be concerned if consuming cardamom as an ingredient in food. If interested in taking medicinal doses, they should first consult with their physician.

Chewing cardamom pods can freshen the breath.

Common Name	Scientific Names	Parts Used	Therapeutic Use
Cardamom	*Elettaria cardamomum* (green cardamom), *Amomum costatum* (black cardamom)	Seeds	Digestive aid

Chamomile

A CALMING CURE

Chamomile is perhaps the most commonly used European herb in herbal medicine today, and has been used over time for relief of nervous tension, muscle cramps, skin conditions, and digestive upsets in babies, children, and adults.

Chamomile is a popular treatment for digestive and inflammatory conditions. In modern herbal medicine, it is suggested for indigestion, heartburn, flatulence, diarrhea, gastritis, infant colic, Crohn's disease, and irritable bowel syndrome. It is recommended to relieve muscle tension and to ease anxiety. Applied externally, chamomile creams soothe irritated or inflamed skin, including eczema. Used as a mouthwash, chamomile has been found to prevent mouth sores associated with chemotherapy and radiation.

Resembling daisies, chamomile flowers can soothe the digestive tract.

▶ OBTAINING AND USING

Chamomile is sold dried and fresh, as well as in capsules, tinctures, and ointments.

Tea: Pour 1 cup boiling water over 1 teaspoon of herb. Steep for 5 to 7 minutes. The longer it steeps, the more powerful its calming effects.

Capsules: Take 500 to 1,000 mg dried chamomile flowers 2 to 3 times a day.

Tincture: Take 3 to 5 ml 2 to 3 times a day.

Topical: Creams are available. Use as directed.

▶ PRECAUTIONS

Chamomile is very safe. In rare cases, allergic reactions occur, especially in those with severe ragweed allergies.

> **RECIPE FOR HEALTH**
>
> **CHAMOMILE COMFORT**
> For a nice soothing pick-me-up in the afternoon, pour 2 cups boiling water over 1 tea bag chamomile, 1 tea bag peppermint, and 1 tea bag green tea. Let the tea bags steep for 5 to 7 minutes. Strain. Drink warm and share with a friend.

Common Name	Scientific Names	Parts Used	Therapeutic Uses
Chamomile	*Matricaria recutita, Chamaemelum nobile*	Dried flower heads, oil	Digestive aid, colic, mouth ulcers

Fennel

DELICIOUS DIGESTIVE

Fennel seeds taste like anise, or licorice.

A close cousin to parsley, caraway, and dill, fennel is a tall plant that can easily reach 4 or 5 feet tall. Its stems arise from a white or pale green bulb that is crunchy and sweet. All parts of fennel are edible and possess a mild flavor similar to anise or licorice.

Contemporary herbalists recommend fennel to relieve bloating, gas, and diarrhea; settle upset stomachs; improve appetite or reduce food cravings; and buffer cramping effects of laxatives. And fennel is still given to infants to relieve colic, gas, and bloating.

▶ HISTORY

Fennel has been a medicinal herb for more than 2,000 years. Roman physician and naturalist Pliny the Elder (A.D. 23–79) included fennel in more than 20 different medicinal remedies. In India, fennel was considered a digestive aid. The emperor Charlemagne (A.D. 742–814) is credited with introducing the herb to central and northern Europe. In England, fennel became one of the nine sacred herbs—described in a 10th-century herbal—believed to cure all illness.

▶ OBTAINING AND USING

Fennel is easily grown from seed sown directly in the garden in a sunny spot. Fennel seed is harvested once the plants ripen. Fennel seed may also be purchased in health food stores. The largest suppliers of fennel seeds to world markets are China, Egypt, and India.

Tea: Pour 1 cup boiling water over 1/2 teaspoon crushed seeds, and steep for 10 minutes and strain. Cool thoroughly if giving to a child.

Common Name	Scientific Name	Parts Used	Therapeutic Uses
Fennel	*Foeniculum vulgare*	Seeds	Digestive aid, colic, stomach cramps

Flaxseed

RELIEF IN TINY PACKAGES

Flaxseeds are the richest known plant source of alpha-linolenic acid (ALA), an omega-3 that may help protect against heart disease and arthritis. Flaxseed is also packed with lignans. In the digestive tract, bacteria convert lignans into estrogen-like molecules that circulate in the body and bind with estrogen receptors on cells. There's some indication this may reduce the risk of certain hormone-related cancers, such as breast cancer, although more research is needed. High in soluble fiber, flaxseed is also good at keeping constipation at bay.

Flaxseed is a wonderful source of fiber and omega-3 fatty acids.

RECIPE FOR HEALTH

FLAX SMOOTHIE
Place 1 to 2 tablespoons of whole flaxseed in a blender and then process until the seeds are ground. Add 1 ripe banana, 1 cup berries (blueberries, strawberries, or raspberries), 1 cup plain yogurt, and 1 tablespoon honey. Blend on high for about 30 to 45 seconds until well mixed.

▸ OBTAINING AND USING

Ripe seeds, powder, capsules, and flaxseed oil are found at health food and grocery stores. After grinding whole flaxseeds, use within 24 hours.

Whole seeds: Grind 1 tablespoon seeds and eat with plenty of water 2 to 3 times daily.

Capsules: Take 1 to 2 daily, or as directed by manufacturer.

Flaxseed oil: Take 1 to 2 tablespoons daily. Liquid flaxseed oil often contains about 7 g of ALA per 15-ml tablespoon, but it does not have the beneficial fiber content of whole seeds and capsules.

▸ PRECAUTIONS

Flaxseed may interact with some prescription medications, so check with your doctor before adding it to your diet. Do not eat raw or unripe flaxseeds—they may be poisonous. Women with breast or ovarian cancers should get their doctor's approval.

Common Name	Scientific Name	Parts Used	Therapeutic Uses
Flaxseed	*Linum usitatissimum*	Seeds	Indigestion, constipation, antioxidant

Goldenseal

A HEALING TREASURE

In modern herbal medicine, goldenseal is recommended for soothing the stomach, aiding digestion, and relieving certain types of diarrhea. It is also used to treat inflammations of the skin, eyes, and mucous membranes, including sinusitis, conjunctivitis, urinary tract infections, vaginitis, sore throats, and canker sores. Many herbalists recommend goldenseal for colds, hay fever (allergic rhinitis), and flu.

▶ OBTAINING AND USING

Supply shortages in the late 1990s and a dramatic rise in the price of the dried root led the U.S. Fish and Wildlife Service to list goldenseal under the CITES treaty, an agreement among nations governing international trade in plants and animals.

Goldenseal is allowed as an export, but exporters must validate that it was obtained in a sustainable manner. Barberry and a root called Oregon grape

Goldenseal roots are a popular remedy for digestive complaints.

root, which like goldenseal have high amounts of berberine, can be used as substitutes with a physician's or expert's approval.

Capsules: Generally, take 1 to 3 g a day.

Tincture: Take 2 to 4 ml, 2 to 3 times a day.

Topical: Salves and ointments are readily available. Use as directed.

▶ PRECAUTIONS

Goldenseal is not recommended for use during pregnancy or breast-feeding. Goldenseal can also interact with enzymes in the body that metabolize certain prescription medications. Those taking other medications should check with their health care professional or pharmacist before taking goldenseal.

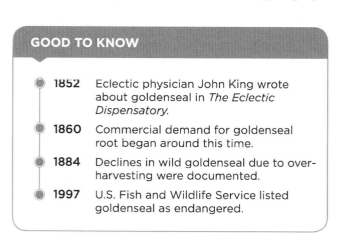

GOOD TO KNOW

1852	Eclectic physician John King wrote about goldenseal in *The Eclectic Dispensatory.*
1860	Commercial demand for goldenseal root began around this time.
1884	Declines in wild goldenseal due to over-harvesting were documented.
1997	U.S. Fish and Wildlife Service listed goldenseal as endangered.

Common Name	Scientific Name	Parts Used	Therapeutic Uses
Goldenseal	*Hydrastis canadensis*	Roots, rhizomes	Digestive aid, diarrhea, anti-inflammatory

Milk Thistle

LIVER'S PROTECTIVE POWERHOUSE

Milk thistle's height, purple flowers, and distinctive white mottled leaves make it stand out visually. Medicinally, it stands out for its ability to gently protect the liver against many toxins.

In the 1960s, interest in milk thistle was rekindled when researchers isolated a complex of chemicals from the herb's seeds with pronounced liver-protecting properties. Compounds in milk thistle called flavonolignans (collectively referred to as silymarin) protect liver cells from damage caused by alcohol and acetaminophen. Milk thistle is recommended to treat symptoms of chronic liver disease and certain types of liver cirrhosis. It can be used to help in treatment with diabetes as well.

No contraindications are associated with this herb, even in substantial dosages. Despite its safety, individuals who have liver disease or are being treated for cancer should discuss the use of any dietary supplement with their health care provider.

Milk thistle is often considered a weed.

▶ OBTAINING AND USING

Milk thistle seeds and extracts are commercially available.

Tea: Simmer 1 teaspoon crushed milk thistle seeds in 1 cup water for 10 minutes. Strain. Drink 1 to 3 cups a day.

Tincture: Alcohol extracts are not advisable if using for liver protection.

Extract: When using milk thistle for liver protection, use a product that contains a minimum 70 percent silymarin. The dose for these products is generally 210 to 420 mg a day.

RECIPE FOR HEALTH

MILK THISTLE SEEDS

Not just for the birds, milk thistle seeds are a good source of protein and amino acids and can be delicious when added to cereals or smoothies. Grind a handful of organic milk thistle seeds and cook with your oatmeal, or substitute milk thistle for flax seeds in recipes.

Common Name	Scientific Name	Parts Used	Therapeutic Use
Milk thistle	*Silybum marianum*	Seeds	Liver protectant

Parsley

MORE THAN JUST A GARNISH

Parsley *(Petroselinum crispum)*

Parsley is one of the world's most widely used herbs. It is an essential ingredient in many dishes. In modern herbal medicine, parsley is suggested to help clear urinary tract disorders, such as cystitis and urethritis. Parsley is also used to treat kidney stones, calm indigestion, and help stimulate normal menstruation. Chewing parsley leaves is also a time-tested method for fresh breath.

▶ OBTAINING AND USING

Fresh parsley is widely available in supermarkets. Health food stores sell tinctures and capsules. Parsley seed is produced on a small scale in eastern Europe.

Tincture: Generally, alcohol extracts, or tinctures, of parsley are dosed at 1 to 2 ml, taken 3 times daily.

Capsules: Take 450 to 900 mg parsley leaf, up to 3 times daily.

Tea: Pour 1 cup boiling water over 1/4 cup (or 2 to 3 tablespoons) fresh parsley leaves. Let stand for 5 minutes, strain, and drink, up to 3 times daily. Tea can be sweetened, if desired.

▶ PRECAUTIONS

High doses of parsley may stimulate both menstrual flow and the uterus so it is not appropriate for pregnant women. The varied effects that parsley has on the kidneys warrant caution in anyone with kidney disease. Also, to prevent an unsafe drop in blood pressure, care should be exercised if parsley is used with high-blood-pressure medications. Parsley may react with sunlight to cause a skin rash.

Common Name	Scientific Name	Parts Used	Therapeutic Uses
Parsley	*Petroselinum crispum*	Leaves, roots, seeds	Digestion, fresh breath, urinary tract health

Peppermint

REFRESHING RELIEF

Peppermint is the aromatic plant that gives the candy of the same name its cool, refreshing taste. It is one of more than two dozen species of mint that belong to the genus *Mentha.*

This herb calms the muscles in the walls of the stomach and intestines. Modern herbal practitioners recommend peppermint for soothing upset stomach or improving digestion; the herb is often used to treat the pain, gas, and diarrhea associated with irritable bowel syndrome. Applied to the skin, peppermint has a cooling effect on rashes, hives, and other irritations. Peppermint is widely used to treat colds and flu, soothe sore throats, and quiet dry coughs.

Peppermint leaves contain oil that is used to flavor candy.

PRECAUTIONS

PEPPERMINT
Do not use peppermint if you have gastroesophageal reflux disease (GERD) or if you have a hiatal hernia, as peppermint can make heartburn worse. Children under two should not use peppermint oil topically as it may cause spasms that inhibit breathing.

▶ OBTAINING AND USING

Peppermint is a long-standing herbal remedy that calms the muscles of the digestive tract and improves the flow of bile from the gallbladder, helping the body digest fat. Peppermint leaves (dried and fresh) as well as lozenges and capsules are available at health food stores.

Tea: Pour 1 cup boiling water over 1 teaspoon dried peppermint leaves, or 6 to 8 fresh leaves. Steep for 10 minutes. Strain and cool. Enjoy 2 to 3 times a day after meals.

Capsules: Take 500 to 1,000 mg dried peppermint leaf after meals. Sustained-release peppermint oil capsules are used for IBS. In studies, 0.2 ml peppermint oil was given 2 to 3 times a day with meals. Only use oil capsules commercially prepared with an enteric coating.

Lozenges: For sore throat and cough, lozenges should contain 5 to 10 mg menthol. Children under two should not be given menthol products.

Common Name	Scientific Name	Parts Used	Therapeutic Uses
Peppermint	*Mentha* x *piperita*	Leaves, oil	Indigestion, irritable bowel syndrome

Psyllium

A MOVER AND A SHAKER

A recommended relief to constipation, psyllium seed husks are an excellent source of soluble fiber that stimulates intestinal contractions and speeds waste through the digestive tract. It has long been used as the primary ingredient in bulk laxatives. Psyllium has been found effective in treating mild to moderate cases of inflammatory bowel disease, irritable bowel syndrome, hemorrhoids, and other intestinal problems. Psyllium appears to effectively lower blood cholesterol levels when added to a low-fat, low-cholesterol diet.

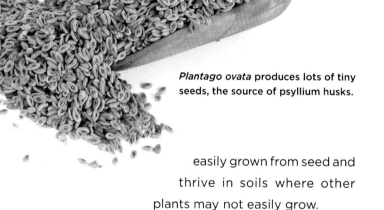

Plantago ovata produces lots of tiny seeds, the source of psyllium husks.

▶ OBTAINING AND USING

Psyllium plants are abundant in many parts of the world and are often regarded as weeds. They are easily grown from seed and thrive in soils where other plants may not easily grow.

Adults: Generally, take 2 to 3 tablespoons a day in divided doses before breakfast and before dinner. Mix each dose in a tall glass of water, stir well, drink, and follow with another glass of water.

Children (younger than 18 years): Generally, take from 1 teaspoon to 1 to 2 tablespoons, depending upon the age and size of the child.

▶ PRECAUTIONS

Obstruction of the gastrointestinal tract has happened in people taking psyllium fiber, particularly if they had undergone previous bowel surgery or when psyllium was taken with inadequate amounts of water. Those who have difficulty swallowing should not take psyllium.

RECIPE FOR HEALTH

PSYLLIUM CHIPS

In a bowl, mix 1/3 cup psyllium husk, 1 tablespoon olive oil, 1 tablespoon Parmesan cheese, and 1 tablespoon sesame seeds. Add 1/2 cup water, stir well, and let sit for 10 minutes. Roll out resulting "dough" to a 1/4-inch thickness on parchment paper and lift onto cookie sheet. Sprinkle with salt (optional). Bake 25 to 30 minutes at 350°F. Cool and break into crunchy chips.

Common Name	Scientific Names	Parts Used	Therapeutic Uses
Psyllium	*Plantago ovata, P. afra*	Seeds, seed husks	Fiber, bulk laxative, heart health

Slippery Elm

GENTLE HEALER

True to its name, this plant is slippery in both taste and texture. Its source is the pleasant-smelling inner bark of *Ulmus rubra,* a medium-size tree native to North America. Slippery elm bark has been used as a food and medicine for centuries.

Slippery elm remains a popular herbal medicine and is widely available. It is one of the few herbs approved by the U.S. Food and Drug Administration, and is sold as a nonprescription drug. Slippery elm helps soothe and heal inflamed mucosal tissues, such as the lining of the throat, stomach, and intestines. Herbal practitioners also suggest it for gastroesophageal reflux disease (GERD), Crohn's disease, ulcerative colitis, and diarrhea.

▶ OBTAINING AND USING

Slippery elm is common in the wild throughout most of its range, so it is seldom cultivated. In the spring,

Slippery elm (*Ulmus rubra*)

the bark can be removed easily in long strips, almost popping off the tree. Most commercial production of slippery elm bark comes from wild populations in Appalachia.

Tea: Add 1 cup boiling water to 1 to 2 teaspoons powdered bark and steep 5 minutes. Drink 2 to 3 times a day.

Capsules: Take 800 to 1,000 mg 3 times daily with a full glass of water. (Capsules can be used to treat diarrhea but won't be helpful for a sore throat.)

Lozenges: Both flavored and unflavored are widely available. Follow the dosing instructions on the label.

GOOD TO KNOW

1787 J. Schoepf listed slippery elm as a "salve bark" in his *Materia Medica Americana.*

1812 U.S. Army troops in the War of 1812 fed horses slippery elm bark when hay ran out.

1847 Thayers Slippery Elm Lozenges, still sold today, appeared on the U.S. market.

1875 Boston schoolmaster George Emerson noted that slippery elm was being overharvested.

Common Name	Scientific Name	Parts Used	Therapeutic Uses
Slippery elm	*Ulmus rubra*	Bark, wood	Heartburn, acid reflux, sore throat

DO IT YOURSELF
Fantastic Healing Foods

What you choose to snack on can really boost your health. Try these four foods and find out:

Awesome Avocado. Avocados are a concentrated source of monounsaturated fat, fiber, and protein (more than any other fruit) as well as potassium and folate, a water-soluble B vitamin that helps prevent changes to DNA that may lead to cancer.

Bravo for Beans. Kidney beans, pinto beans, lentils, and other varieties offer a bonanza of vitamins and are low in fat but rich in protein.

Berry Good. Blueberries, raspberries, strawberries, cranberries, and other berries contain potent antioxidants called anthocyanins, providing powerful protection against the types of cell damage thought to lead to cancer, heart disease, and age-related memory loss.

Nuts for Nuts. Nuts are loaded with protein, high in fiber, full of vitamins and minerals, and yes, rich sources of unsaturated fat. Moderation is key: A small handful—about an ounce—can provide dramatic health benefits for less than 200 calories a day.

HEALTHY HOMEMADE GUACAMOLE

When made with fresh ingredients and enjoyed in moderation, this traditional Mexican dip is a healthy way to get fiber, monounsaturated fat (aka the "good" kind), beta-carotene, thiamine, vitamin C, riboflavin, and potassium. To make your own at home, cut 3 Haas avocados in half, remove the pit, and scoop out the flesh. In a bowl, mash the avocado flesh with 1/4 cup chopped, fresh cilantro, 3 tablespoons diced red onion, the juice of a lime, and 1 diced jalapeño pepper. Add salt and pepper to taste.

CHAPTER FIVE

FEELING STRONG

JOINTS AND MUSCLES

Muscles, bones, and joints form the crux of our internal support system. These components protect our internal organs while allowing our bodies to move in myriad ways. Tissues called ligaments bind our bones together at joints, while tendons anchor muscles to bones. Muscles come in three forms: skeletal, cardiac, and smooth. Good nutrition and exercise are vital to keeping these important parts of the body strong.

Age and use are rarely kind to these structures. For all their strength and flexibility, they can be damaged. Muscles can be overstretched, bruised, or torn. Bones can be weakened, tendons bruised and torn. Joints can be strained, sprained, or dislocated. They are also targets for inflammatory, degenerative, and autoimmune diseases, such as osteoarthritis and rheumatoid arthritis.

Ancient healers invariably turned to plants for solutions to these problems, often applying herbal preparations to the skin. Many herbs are still used by modern practitioners.

Opposite: Vibrant dried goji berries are a colorful way to better health.
Above: Comfrey *(Symphytum officinale)*

Arnica

A BALM FOR BRUISES

An athlete's best friend, *Arnica montana* grows high in the mountains, native to sunny alpine meadows of Europe, Central Asia, and Siberia. Sporting deep yellow, daisy-like flowers, arnica has been prized for centuries in these regions for its ability to ease the pain and inflammation of sore muscles, bruises, and sprains.

Popular in Europe, *Arnica montana* is currently an ingredient in more than a hundred German herbal preparations. Originally, the entire plant, including the roots, was used in preparing herbal remedies, but now typically only the flower heads are used.

▶ HISTORY

Long before the healing properties of arnica were recognized in Europe, the herb was used there in pagan rituals designed to ensure a good harvest. By the 1500s, interest in arnica had shifted from the magical to the medicinal. Italian physician and herbalist Pietro Andrea Mattioli wrote favorably about the herb's healing properties in his botanical masterpiece, *Commentarii in Sex Libros Pedacii Dioscoridis,* which was first published in 1544.

In North America, Native Americans used related species, such as *Arnica fulgens,* to treat bruising,

Yellow blossoms of arnica can treat bruises, strains, and swelling.

muscle soreness, and back pain. Arnica found a place in the folk medicine of many other European countries, especially Germany and Austria, where it remains an important medicinal herb to this day.

▶ OBTAINING AND USING

Preparations of this herb are sold in stores—as gels, ointments, creams, and sprays—for external use in treating bruises, muscle strains, sprains and dislocations, arthritis and rheumatic pain, phlebitis, and swelling due to fractures. Arnica salves can be effective remedies for chapped lips and acne. Tinctures of arnica are also common for use as bases in making compresses and poultices.

Commercially available arnica is obtained from both wild and cultivated sources. In the United States, much of the material is collected in the wild from Montana, Wyoming, and the Dakotas. *Arnica montana* is grown in parts of Europe and in northern India. Arnica is sold in health food stores as tablets, tinctures, ointments, gels, and mouth rinses. Store arnica in a cool, dry

Dried arnica flowers

place, away from humidity and direct sunlight. **Creams, gels, ointments, and salves:** Arnica topicals can be applied to an injury several times daily, or follow product instructions. Commercial arnica topical preparations are widely available.

Poultice: Steep 3 tablespoons arnica flowers in a cup of hot water. Let stand for 10 minutes. Cool and apply saturated plant material to injury for 10 to 15 minutes. Repeat 3 to 4 times daily for an acute injury.

▶ PRECAUTIONS

Arnica should not be taken internally. It can cause heart arrhythmias and possible respiratory collapse; this concern is avoided with homeopathic preparations, because the arnica has been significantly diluted. Applied externally, arnica is generally safe and is usually well tolerated; if a rash should appear, discontinue use.

HOW TO HARVEST

Two species are found in Europe and one in Japan. The vast majority of arnicas, 26 in all, grow in western North America, ranging from Canada to Mexico. Arnica plants are locally protected in the wild, and the harvest of wild plants is discouraged. As a predominantly subalpine to alpine plant group, arnicas succeed in cool climates and poor, acidic soils. Propagation is by root division early in the season or by seeds. The daisy-like flowers are yellow to yellow-orange. All of the aboveground parts, harvested in flower, are used in herbal medicine.

Common Name	Scientific Name	Parts Used	Therapeutic Uses
Arnica	*Arnica montana*	Flowers, leaves	Bruises, contusions, swelling, joint pain

Cat's Claw

SMOOTH MOVER

Cat's claw is a large vine native to tropical regions of South and Central America that flourishes in the rain forest canopy. This agile plant anchors itself to tree trunks and branches as it climbs more than a hundred feet. Today, cat's claw is thought to be a powerful stimulator of the immune system with potent anti-inflammatory properties. Herbalists use cat's claw to treat joint problems, such as osteoarthritis and rheumatoid arthritis.

RECIPE FOR HEALTH

CAT'S CLAW TEA
To make cat's claw tea, simply add 1 teaspoon cat's claw root bark to 4 cups boiling water. Stir well and pour into a saucepan with a tight-fitting lid. Simmer this mixture for 10 to 15 minutes. Cool, strain, and drink 1 cup approximately 3 times a day.

▶ OBTAINING AND USING
Dosages depend on which of the two species are used and how the product is prepared. Follow manufacturer's dosage guidelines. The following preparations apply to *U. tomentosa:*

Tea: Boil 1 g root bark for 15 minutes in 250 ml water (about a cup). The decoction is strained, cooled, and taken 1 to 3 times a day.

Tincture: Take 1 to 2 ml, 2 to 3 times daily.

Extract: Dried, powdered extracts are mixed into water; follow product label instructions.

Capsules: Capsules of cat's claw contain standardized amounts of alkaloids or other compounds. Follow manufacturer's instructions.

Cat's claw bark and roots are believed to ease stiffness and soreness in the joints.

▶ PRECAUTIONS
Mild side effects from cat's claw may include stomach upset, headache, and dizziness. Those with autoimmune diseases or those taking immunosuppressive medications or blood pressure medicines should not use cat's claw. Do not take if pregnant or nursing.

Common Name	Scientific Name	Parts Used	Therapeutic Uses
Cat's claw	*Uncaria tomentosa*	Bark, roots	Osteoarthritis, rheumatoid arthritis

Cayenne

BRINGING THE HEAT

Spicy cuisines often share an ingredient: hot cayenne pepper. These peppers get their heat from a plant chemical called capsaicin, which also has pain-relieving properties.

Cayenne is added to lotions and salves to relieve the pain of osteoarthritis and rheumatoid arthritis, shingles, and fibromyalgia-related joint or muscle pain and to reduce itching and inflammation associated with psoriasis. Concentrated capsaicin creams (often available only with prescription) are sometimes used for postsurgical pain and certain types of neuropathy.

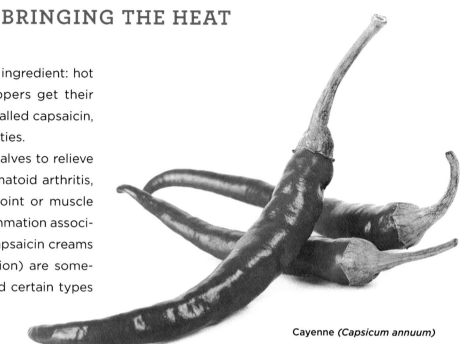

Cayenne *(Capsicum annuum)*

▶ OBTAINING AND USING

Topical creams containing capsaicin are widely available for purchase, some with prescription.

Cream: For nerve-related pain, apply a cream containing 0.075 percent capsaicin 3 to 4 times daily. Lower-dose creams containing only 0.025 percent capsaicin applied 4 times daily may be effective for arthritis. For optimal benefit, treatment is usually recommended for 6 to 8 weeks; benefits for arthritis may occur before 8 weeks. Researchers are developing other higher-dose forms of cayenne.

▶ PRECAUTIONS

Application of cayenne preparations to the skin can cause a rash as well as burning, stinging, and redness. The rash, often an irritation rather than an allergic reaction, is usually worse on first applications of the preparation and then gets better with repeated use. However, if the rash gets worse with time, discontinue use. Wash hands thoroughly and keep preparation well away from eyes or sensitive skin. Do not apply to broken skin.

RECIPE FOR HEALTH

CAYENNE LEMONADE

At the first signs of a cold, or if you're simply feeling the chills or aches on a bitter winter day, try this peppery treat. Combine 1 cup boiling water, the juice of 1 lemon, and 2 to 3 dashes dried ground cayenne. Stir well, sweeten to taste with honey or stevia—and let this zingy drink perk you up.

Common Name	Scientific Name	Parts Used	Therapeutic Use
Cayenne	*Capsicum annuum*	Fruits	Arthritis, nerve pain

Cinquefoil

A FIVE-SIDED MEDICINE

Cinquefoil leaves have five leaflets.

Cinquefoil is a healing herb that has many names—a scientific one, *Potentilla reptans,* and common names like five fingers, five-leaf grass, and creeping cinquefoil. It is a creeping plant with large yellow flowers and leaves divided into five leaflets.

Cinquefoil has been traditionally used as an anti-inflammatory, an astringent, and an antihemorrhagic agent. It was also a very common remedy for treating fevers, but this has been questioned due to studies not finding evidence to support these claims.

▶ HISTORY

Cinquefoil's history of medicinal use goes all the way back to ancient Greece. Theophrastus, a philosopher and naturalist, first documented the beneficial effects of the plant. Herbalists through the ages recommended the herb's root for fevers and pain relief.

▶ OBTAINING AND USING

Dried cinquefoil is available for sale, but the plant is also easily grown. The best time to harvest and collect cinquefoil is at the peak of summer. Only harvest undamaged parts and then dry the plant in a cool, dark place.

Infusion: Use 1 teaspoon dried cinquefoil in 1 cup boiling water. Steep for 30 minutes; strain and drink up to 3 times a day.

▶ PRECAUTIONS

Cinquefoil seems to be safe for most adults. Not enough is known about use during pregnancy and breast-feeding, so avoid use.

Common Name	Scientific Name	Parts Used	Therapeutic Uses
Cinquefoil	*Potentilla reptans*	Flowers, leaves, roots	Anti-inflammatory, mouth sores

Comfrey

REPAIRING AND RESTORING

Colloquial names such as knitbone, boneset, and bruisewort reflect comfrey's use as a topical treatment through many centuries to promote healing of bruises, sprains, strains, and pulls. Recently, comfrey has shown promise for relieving acute upper or lower back pain.

▶ OBTAINING AND USING

Comfrey ointments, creams, poultices, and liniments are applied to heal bruises, ease sore muscles, and speed the healing of injuries.

Cream, gel, or ointment: Germany's Commission E authorities recommend no more than 1 mg

Comfrey leaves are covered with rough bristles.

SOOTHING COMFREY SALVE
Mix 1 cup olive oil with 1 tablespoon each dried comfrey leaves, lavender flowers, and calendula petals. Stir in the top of a double boiler for 40 minutes. Cool, strain, and reserve oil. Melt 1/4 cup beeswax in the double boiler. Stir in strained oil. Pour into salve tins.

comfrey daily to limit toxicity to the liver and other organs. Concerns over comfrey's toxicity are addressed by using specialized formulations where the dangerous alkaloids have been removed and the anti-inflammatory and pain-relieving substances retained.

Extracts: Brands guaranteed to be free of pyrrolizidine alkaloids are the safest. These preparations can be massaged into affected joints 3 to 4 times daily.

▶ PRECAUTIONS

Comfrey leaf and root contain liver toxins and cancer-causing compounds potentially dangerous when ingested or applied to the skin. Use only topical preparations of comfrey that have been purified of their toxic pyrrolizidine alkaloids. Preparations free of these compounds are presumed safer, though most sources still warn against applying comfrey products on open wounds.

Common Name	Scientific Name	Parts Used	Therapeutic Use
Comfrey	*Symphytum officinale*	Leaves, roots	Joint pain

Corn Silk

A THROWAWAY CURE

Corn on the cob is a delicious summertime staple. After shucking corn, most people throw away the corn silk without knowing it's an effective natural treatment for bumps, bruises, and even bladder infections. Dried corn silk has a diuretic effect, which herbalists believe helps the body flush out excess toxins and waste. Herbalists today recommend it for urinary tract health, including infections and bed-wetting. It is also recommended for reducing inflammation.

▶ HISTORY

Grown in North and South America, corn silk was used by the Maya, Inca, and other Native American peoples to treat bruises, sores, and rashes. Corn

Although most people throw it away, corn silk has many uses and healthful properties.

silk teas were used to tread bladder infections and urethritis as well.

▶ OBTAINING AND USING

Corn silk supplements, extracts, and capsules are readily available at health food stores. You can also make your own by saving the corn silk after shucking corn on the cob. Collect the strands and lay them flat on a paper towel to dry. Store in a cool, dry place before use.

Tea: Add 1 tablespoon chopped corn silk to 1 cup water, just off the boil. Cover and steep for 15 to 20 minutes or until cool enough to drink. Strain and drink 2 to 3 times a day.

▶ PRECAUTIONS

Corn silk seems to be safe for most people. Anyone with a corn allergy should avoid using it.

Common Name	Scientific Name	Parts Used	Therapeutic Uses
Corn silk	*Zea mays*	Dried corn silk	Bruises, swelling, rashes

Dandelion

MEDICINE IN DISGUISE

Most people see dandelions as pests. But herbalists see them as treasures packed with protein, fiber, calcium, phosphorus, iron, potassium, thiamin, riboflavin, vitamin C, and vitamin A. Herbalists recommend dandelion to stimulate the appetite; protect the kidneys, liver, and gall bladder; and as a powerful anti-inflammatory.

▶ HISTORY

Dandelions historically have been used for many ailments. Europeans used them to treat fever, boils, eye problems, diabetes, and diarrhea. Native Americans used them to treat kidney disease, swelling, skin

DANDELION TEA
Combine 2 tablespoons dried dandelion root, 2 tablespoons dried dandelion leaves, 3 teaspoons fennel seeds, and 3 teaspoons dried peppermint with 1 cup boiling water. Steep for 10 minutes, strain, and sip for relief of stomachache.

problems, heartburn, and upset stomach. In traditional Chinese medicine, dandelion has been used to treat stomach problems, appendicitis, and breast problems, such as inflammation or lack of milk flow.

▶ OBTAINING AND USING

Dried dandelion leaves and roots are widely available, as are teas, capsules, tablets, tinctures, and extracts made from them.

Leaf tincture: Take 30 to 60 drops, 3 times daily.
Root tincture: Take 30 to 60 drops, 3 times daily.

▶ PRECAUTIONS

Dandelion is generally considered safe, but anyone with a ragweed allergy should avoid it. Those with kidney problems, gallbladder problems, or gallstones should ask their health care provider before eating dandelion. If harvesting wild dandelions, take care to find clean plants that have not been sprayed with weed killer or other herbicides that are not safe for consumption.

Despite their reputation as pests, dandelions are valuable medicinal plants.

Common Name	Scientific Name	Parts Used	Therapeutic Uses
Dandelion	*Taraxacum officinale*	Leaves, roots	Joint paint, muscle aches, digestive aid, diuretic

Goji

FEEL-GOOD FRUITS

Products containing goji berries often feature extravagant claims of health benefits that sound too good to be true. Research into specific benefits of goji berries is ongoing, but what is known is that goji berries are rich in antioxidants. Goji juice may also be a mild adaptogen.

▶ OBTAINING AND USING

Most of the commercial goji berry supply sold in the United States is from China; goji is widely cultivated and found in bulk in every market in central and western Asia.

Sweet-tart goji berries are nutrient dense.

<table>
<tr><td>GOOD TO KNOW</td></tr>
<tr><td>

• Goji has been cultivated along China's Yellow River since the 1400s.

• Goji berries are considered both a fruit and an herb.

• In 2004, China exported $120 million worth of goji berries and products.

• Goji berries are also called wolfberries.

</td></tr>
</table>

Juice: Goji juice is kept refrigerated until use. One clinical trial used 120 ml of the juice as a daily serving, considered a standard dose in traditional Chinese medicine.

Tea: In Chinese medicine, a water-based extract (the equivalent of 2 tablespoons dried root bark per 1/2 cup water) is used daily for high blood pressure, while 1/3 to 1/2 that dose is used daily for diabetes.

Capsules: Take 500 mg, 1 to 3 times daily.

▶ PRECAUTIONS

Goji should be avoided by those undergoing chemotherapy or radiation therapy unless recommended by a health care provider. Those taking high blood pressure or diabetes medicines should also seek advice before taking. Goji may increase the activity of blood-thinning medications such as warfarin; avoid combining these.

Common Name	Scientific Names	Parts Used	Therapeutic Uses
Goji	*Lycium barbarum, L. chinense*	Fruit	Anti-inflammatory, general well-being

Turmeric

A COLORFUL CURE

Turmeric *(Curcuma longa)*

Turmeric is used to treat joint pain, digestive and liver problems, and skin conditions. Herbalists recommend turmeric for indigestion and diarrhea, as well as inflammatory bowel conditions. Other uses include clearing up skin conditions such as eczema and psoriasis, preventing cardiovascular disease and cancer, and reducing blood cholesterol levels.

▶ HISTORY

Turmeric has been used in Indian Ayurvedic and Unani traditional medicine for at least 2,500 years, primarily to treat digestive and liver disorders, skin infections and irritations, and arthritis. In China, traditional medical practitioners prescribed turmeric for abdominal pain, jaundice, and menstrual conditions.

▶ OBTAINING AND USING

Turmeric makes an excellent container plant for a patio, and can be bought from nurseries specializing in herbs.

Tea: Pour 2 cups boiling water over 1 teaspoon turmeric and steep for 10 minutes. Strain.

Capsules: Take 2 to 3 g turmeric a day for 60 to 100 mg curcumin, the daily amount typically consumed in the Indian diet.

Standardized extract: Purchase an extract that guarantees a specific level of curcumin (sometimes written as curcuminoid on the label). Most studies used turmeric extracts providing 1 to 2 g a day of curcumin, taken in 2 to 3 divided doses. Curcumin doesn't readily absorb in the body on its own, so it's helpful to add some kind of fat, such as coconut milk. Many brands also add piperine, a pepper extract, to enhance absorption.

Common Name	Scientific Name	Parts Used	Therapeutic Uses
Turmeric	*Curcuma longa*	Roots, rhizomes	Muscle pain, rheumatoid arthritis, digestive aid

Willow Bark

A BARK TO CURE THE BITE

White willow bark *(Salix alba)*, along with the closely related basket willow *(S. purpurea)* and crack willow *(S. fragilis)*, is a rich source of salicin, a chemical converted in the body to salicylic acid, a close relative to one of the most widely used drugs in the world: aspirin. Recent studies confirm that willow bark contains other compounds with antioxidant, antiseptic, and immune-boosting properties. In modern herbal medicine, willow bark is recommended for back pain, osteoarthritis and rheumatism pain, sprains, toothache, headache, fever, colds, and flu.

▶ OBTAINING AND USING

The level of salicin varies considerably from one

Willow bark *(Salix alba)*

GOOD TO KNOW	
Fourth century B.C.	Hippocrates noted using willow bark and leaves for headaches, pain, and fever.
A.D. **1838**	Italian chemist R. Piria, at the Sorbonne in Paris, converted salicin into salicylic acid.
1853	French chemist C. Gerhardt created acetylsalicylic acid but abandoned his discovery.
1899	German chemist F. Hoffmann unearthed Gerhardt's formula, and aspirin was born.

species of willow to another, so the level of pain relief may vary between teas and products.

Tea: Simmer 1 teaspoon willow bark in 1 cup water for 10 minutes. Strain. Add honey to taste, if desired. Drink 1 cup 2 to 3 times a day.

Extracts: Buy a willow bark product standardized to salicin; take a daily dose equivalent to 120 to 240 mg salicin, in 2 or 3 doses. It may take a week to see benefits.

▶ PRECAUTIONS

The risks of willow bark may be similar to those of aspirin; thus, its use is contraindicated in children with fever to avoid the risk of Reye's syndrome. Use is also contraindicated for women who are pregnant or breast-feeding and for people with allergies.

Common Name	Scientific Names	Parts Used	Therapeutic Uses
Willow bark	*Salix alba, S. purpurea, S. fragilis*	Bark	Headache, back pain, osteoarthritis

DO IT YOURSELF
Massage Therapy

Self-massage techniques can release tension, loosen cramped muscles, and ease away stress. To perform any of these techniques, sit in a quiet comfortable place and lubricate your fingers with a little oil.

De-Stress Shoulders. Reach for the area between your left shoulder and your neck with your right hand. (Use your left hand to support your right arm at the elbow.) Firmly squeeze and knead the large band of muscle and tissue that runs between your neck and the end of your collarbone. Massage slowly back and forth for a minute or two, and then switch sides.

Help Your Hands. Use your right thumb and index finger to gently squeeze and knead the fleshy areas between the fingers and thumb of your left hand. Then squeeze each finger, working from the knuckle toward the fingertip. Finally, using your thumb, make firm circling motions all over the palm. Repeat the same procedure on your right hand.

HANDS-ON MASSAGE OIL

For a relaxing massage, mix 2 to 3 drops lavender essential oil with 1 tablespoon sweet almond oil, grape seed oil, or jojoba oil. Use this oil mixture to give your arms, hands, legs, and feet a calming massage treatment.

GLOWING COMPLEXION

THE SKIN

Thin, stretchy, and relatively tough, skin is far more than just a veneer. With minute receptors for touch, pressure, and pain, skin is a sensor, monitoring the body's surroundings and everything it contacts. With tiny blood vessels, sweat glands, and hairs, skin also acts as a thermostat, ready to release heat or conserve it to regulate body temperature. Skin is also a watertight barrier and shield, the first line of defense against the outside world. For all its toughness, however, skin can be easily bruised, burned, and abraded in everyday life. It can erupt with welts, rashes, hives, and sores as a result of allergies, disease, exposure, and stress.

Ancient healers invariably turned to plants for solutions to these problems. Skin conditions were often treated with oils pressed from plant leaves or fruits, salves made from mixing plant parts with fats, and infusions brewed by steeping herbs in hot water. Today, modern herbalists still turn to plants to cleanse, heal, and soothe the skin.

Opposite: Yellow calendula is nicknamed "pot marigold."
Above: Rosemary *(Rosmarinus officinalis)*

Aloe

SUPERB SKIN HEALER

Native to North Africa and coastal areas surrounding the Mediterranean Sea, aloe is one of the most familiar of all herbal remedies. A leaf plucked from the plant and sliced open shelters at its core a clear mucilaginous gel remarkably effective for soothing wounds and burns, speeding healing, and reducing risk of infection. Applied externally, it provides immediate relief for burns, sunburn, skin irritations, scrapes, and minor wounds. It is useful in soothing outbreaks of genital herpes and psoriasis. Aloe gel contains active compounds that decrease pain and inflammation and stimulate skin repair. Aloe gel and aloe juice (from aloe gel) are taken internally for osteoarthritis, stomach ulcers, irritable bowel syndrome, and asthma. Studies suggest that aloe juice may help lower blood sugar and speed wound healing in those with diabetes.

▶ HISTORY

Aloe vera has been cultivated for thousands of years, obscuring with certainty its geographical origin. A commonly accepted theory is that aloe vera originated in the Canary Islands and was brought to the

A worker harvests leaves on an aloe farm.

Mediterranean region by early seafaring traders. The plant was found throughout the Mediterranean region some 2,000 years ago. Dioscorides, a physician in the Roman army of Nero, mentioned it in his medical compendium, *De Materia Medica.*

A recent study theorizes that *A. vera* may have originated in the southern Arabian Peninsula, once a key trading point for medicinal plants in the ancient world, and subsequently spread through the Egyptian empire. In ancient Egypt, aloe was known as the plant of immortality. Greek philosopher Aristotle is said to have urged his student Alexander the Great to claim a group of islands off the Horn of Africa to acquire the aloes that grew there for his army's medicinal arsenal. Legend has it that Cleopatra massaged aloe gel into her skin as part of her daily beauty routine. Aloe found its way into European herbal medicine by the 10th century. The gel was applied externally to soothe and heal wounds and maintain healthy skin. Herbalists prescribed it internally for stomach disorders, insomnia, hemorrhoids, headaches, gum diseases, and kidney ailments. Aloe latex was prescribed for constipation.

▸ OBTAINING AND USING

Today aloe is the most common medicinal plant grown in American households. Many consider it most effective when taken directly from fresh-cut leaves, but it is also a common ingredient in over-the-counter skin care products.

Aloe gel: Apply to the skin several times daily for burns and other skin conditions. For colitis, take 25 to 30 ml (about 2 tablespoons) twice daily; for diabetes, take 10 to 20 ml (about 1 tablespoon) daily. Follow manufacturer's guidelines. Note: Aloe juice should not be taken for colitis.

HOW TO HARVEST

Aloe plants grow well in arid climates with gravelly, well-drained, infertile soil. They require little water and lots of sun. On aloe plantations, commercially raised plants grow in fields of long rows—some 5,000 plants per acre. Aloe harvesting typically takes place four times a year, with two to three of a plant's outer leaves removed each time. Machine processing of freshly harvested leaves has largely replaced traditional methods. Large-scale commercial cultivation occurs in south Texas and Mexico, supplying cosmetic and dietary supplement markets worldwide.

▸ PRECAUTIONS

Topically applied, aloe is safe. It is important to buy aloe gel that says it is made from the inner fillet and/or that it is free of aloin. Aloe juice containing aloin can act as a laxative and can irritate the intestines. Prolonged use can lead to electrolyte loss and dependence on juice for normal bowel function. Those with acute or severe gastrointestinal symptoms should not take the juice. Children and pregnant or nursing women should not take aloe internally.

Common Name	Scientific Name	Parts Used	Therapeutic Uses
Aloe	*Aloe vera*	Leaves	Burns, psoriasis, colitis

Avocado

BUTTERY-SOFT SKIN

Avocados are sometimes called "butter pears," a nickname that suits their distinction of being the world's fattiest fruits—incredibly rich sources of healthful monounsaturated fat. Avocados are also good sources of fiber and protein (more than any other fruit) as well as potassium and folate, a water-soluble B vitamin that helps prevent changes to DNA that may lead to cancer.

Rich in oil and vitamins, avocado is an old remedy for soothing skin irritations and moisturizing dry skin. Some use avocado to relieve symptoms of psoriasis, eczema, and athlete's foot, although more scientific research needs to be done to fully support those claims.

Avocado (Persea americana)

▶ OBTAINING AND USING

Avocados are native to Central and South America, where people have been growing them for millennia. Archaeologists have found avocado seeds buried with Inca mummies in Peru dating back to 750 B.C. Avocados were cultivated in Mexico as early as 500 B.C. The fatty fruit is an excellent food source. It is widely available for sale in grocery stores everywhere and can be used to make skin care treatments at home. Skin and hair care products containing avocado are widespread as well.

Dry skin: Mash a few slices of ripe avocado and apply it directly to the skin. Leave on for 20 minutes, and then rinse clean.

▶ PRECAUTIONS

When eaten in food amounts, avocado is safe for most people. Its high calorie count makes it important to consume in moderation.

RECIPE FOR HEALTH

AVOCADO & MELON SMOOTHIE
Combine the flesh of 1 ripe Haas avocado with 1 cup cantaloupe melon chunks, juice from 1 lime, 1 cup almond or soy milk, 1 cup fat-free plain yogurt, and 1/2 cup orange juice. Process in a blender until smooth. Serve cold.

Common Name	Scientific Name	Parts Used	Therapeutic Uses
Avocado	*Persea americana*	Fruit, oil	Skin care, athlete's foot

Calendula

POWER FLOWER FOR THE SKIN

For a pretty little plant, calendula packs a big, healthy punch by making the skin heal faster. Herbalists recommend calendula lotions, creams, and ointments for chapped skin, eczema, minor cuts and burns, diaper rash, insect bites, hemorrhoids, athlete's foot, and varicose veins.

Taken internally, calendula may relieve throat infections, improve digestion, and heal gastric and duodenal ulcers. Recently, calendula topical ointment has been shown to help prevent dermatitis in breast cancer patients undergoing radiation.

▶ HISTORY

Medicinally, calendula petals have been used since at least the 12th century. Traditionally, preparations were administered internally for fevers, stomach upsets, ulcers, and more. Calendula's chief use, however, was external, as a remedy for

Calendula has been cultivated for centuries.

skin conditions and for infection in minor wounds.

▶ OBTAINING AND USING

Calendula is cultivated in gardens worldwide from subarctic regions to the tropics. The flowers and the whole plant are used in herbal medicine. The whole plant is harvested fresh for tinctures and extracts. Usually the dried flower heads are used in teas.

Topical preparations: Extracts are incorporated into many skin products: soaps, creams, ointments, salves, and lotions with various concentrations of calendula. Apply preparations 3 to 4 times daily to heal minor skin conditions.

GOOD TO KNOW

1100s	Calendula was cultivated in European gardens.
1477	Macer's herbal claimed the herb improves eyesight, draws out "wicked humours."
1699	*The Countrie Farme* noted calendula helps "headache, jaundice, red eyes and ague."
1860s	Calendula was used by field doctors during the American Civil War to staunch bleeding.

Common Name	Scientific Name	Parts Used	Therapeutic Uses
Calendula	*Calendula officinalis*	Flowers	Dry skin, dermatitis, cuts, abrasions

Coconut Oil

THE SKIN'S BEST FRIEND

Many people associate coconuts with pleasure and relaxation, but coconut oil is also a great natural remedy for all sorts of skin problems: dry skin, itchiness, athlete's foot, ringworm, diaper rash, and eczema. The oil contains lauric acid, which gives it antiviral and antifungal properties. One other promising area is hair care, and studies have shown coconut oil to be very effective in getting rid of lice.

Recently, coconut oil has become something of a miracle cure with claims for everything from weight loss to heart disease. Many of these claims are being researched, but one area is not in dispute: skin care.

Coconut oil is extracted from the "meat" of mature coconuts.

> **RECIPE FOR HEALTH**
>
> ### LICE TREATMENT
> Wet hair with a bottle of apple cider vinegar and let it air-dry. Pour liquid coconut oil on the head, completely saturating the hair and scalp. Cover with a shower cap and leave on for 10 to 12 hours. Use a nit comb to remove eggs and dead lice. Wash out the rest of the oil with regular shampoo.

▶ HISTORY

Coconuts grow on palm trees found in tropical areas all over the world. Scientists believe that they were first cultivated in two main locations: the islands in Southeast Asia and the coast and coastal islands of India. Ancient peoples used coconuts for many things: food, fuel, and medicine.

▶ OBTAINING AND USING

Some coconut oil labels describe it as "virgin," but note that, unlike olive oil, no industry standard exists for that term. It generally means that the oil is unprocessed. Coconut oil can be stored at room temperature without spoiling. It will solidify below 76°F.

For skin care: Take a dime-size amount of coconut oil and massage daily into your hands, arms, legs, and feet.

Common Name	Scientific Name	Parts Used	Therapeutic Uses
Coconut	*Cocos nucifera*	Oil	Moisturizer, hair care

Goldenrod

MAKING THE SKIN WHOLE

Goldenrod flowers are used to treat a number of skin conditions.

Goldenrod has been traditionally used in a number of ways: for pain, urinary tract health, arthritis treatment, and relief from eczema and other skin conditions. A few animal and test-tube studies support its use to help reduce inflammation, relieve muscle spasms, fight infections, and lower blood pressure. It does seem to act like a diuretic, and is used in Europe to treat urinary tract inflammation and to prevent or treat kidney stones.

HISTORY

Goldenrod's genus, *Solidago,* means "to make whole," and that is what goldenrod has been doing since antiquity. Many species are native to North America. Native Americans used the plant leaves to make topical treatments for wound healing, relief from eczema, arthritis, and rheumatism. In folk medicine, it is used as a mouth rinse to treat inflammation of the mouth and throat.

OBTAINING AND USING

Goldenrod is available in a number of forms including as a cream, ointment, extract, and dried herb (for teas and in capsules).

Cream: Apply topically and follow manufacturer's recommendations.

Tea: Pour 1 cup boiling water over 1 teaspoon dried goldenrod. Steep for 5 to 10 minutes and drink. The mixture can be cooled and gargled as a mouthwash.

PRECAUTIONS

People with kidney problems should consult a physician before using goldenrod.

Common Name	Scientific Names	Parts Used	Therapeutic Uses
Goldenrod	*Solidago canadensis, S. virgaurea*	Leaves, stems, flowers	Wound healing, astringent, diuretic

Grindelia

POWER AGAINST POISON IVY

Some plants are healers, and others are not. Poison ivy, poison oak, and poison sumac are three of the latter. These notorious three-leaved plants contain an oil, urushiol, that causes people's skin to break out in an itchy, blistering rash. For relief, people can turn to another plant: grindelia. Sometimes called "gumweed," grindelia has been shown to be very effective at treating rashes caused by these poisonous plants by calming the itch and healing the skin.

▶ HISTORY

Native to North and South America, grindelia was widely used to treat bronchitis and asthma, in addition to many different skin afflictions, including reactions

Grindelia can heal the oozy rash caused by poison ivy.

to poison ivy. Western practitioners did not recognize grindelia's healing abilities until the mid-19th century, when it became a popular medicinal herb.

▶ OBTAINING AND USING

Dried and powdered flowers are sold, as are tinctures and capsules. Grindelia-containing ointments and scrubs are sold to treat exposure to poison ivy.

Tincture: Apply a thin layer to areas of the skin exposed to poison ivy or poison oak about 4 times a day.

Infusion: For relief from cold and cough symptoms, pour 1 cup boiling water onto 1 teaspoon dried grindelia. Infuse for 10 to 15 minutes. Drink 2 to 3 times daily.

▶ PRECAUTIONS

Few side effects are reported for grindelia use, making it safe for most people. However, women who are pregnant or nursing should avoid it.

Common Name	Scientific Names	Parts Used	Therapeutic Uses
Grindelia	*Grindelia camporum, G. robusta*	Flowering tops, leaves	Poison ivy/poison oak reactions, upper respiratory infections

Lavender

THE SCENT THAT SOOTHES

When one is feeling stressed out and anxious, the scent of lavender relaxes and soothes. It has long been used to ease stress and insomnia. Lavender also has a long history of skin care usage. Throughout the Mediterranean world, India, and Tibet, lavender was valued for its disinfecting and antiseptic properties as well as its aroma. Today, herbalists still recommend lavender for minor skin ailments, such as fungal infections, cuts and scrapes, and even eczema.

▶ OBTAINING AND USING

Lavender first grew in mountainous zones of the Mediterranean, but today it flourishes throughout southern Europe, Australia, and the United States. A popular choice for gardeners, it is also widely available for purchase as whole dried flowers, essential oils, teas, tinctures, and extracts.

Topical oil: Mix 3 to 5 drops lavender essential oil

Lavender
(*Lavandula angustifolia*)

with 1 teaspoon sweet almond or grape seed oil. To treat fungal infections, like athlete's foot, and bug bites, rub into affected area twice a day.

Infusion: Steep 1 tablespoon dried flowers in a cup of just boiled water for 15 minutes. Cool and strain the liquid. It can be used as a compress (hold over affected area for 15 minutes) or dabbed on cuts and scrapes as a mild antiseptic.

▶ PRECAUTIONS

In general, lavender is safe for use by most people, but some have reported irritation when it is applied to the skin. Lavender's essential oil is toxic if taken orally.

RECIPE FOR HEALTH

LAVENDER SALVE

Put 1/4 cup shea butter, 1 tablespoon sweet almond oil, and 4 teaspoons grated beeswax in the top of a double boiler. Warm slowly to melt the ingredients. Remove from heat and add 12 drops lavender oil and the contents of a vitamin E capsule. Stir until thoroughly combined. Store in a small dark glass jar with a tight-fitting lid.

Common Name	Scientific Name	Parts Used	Therapeutic Uses
Lavender	*Lavandula angustifolia*	Flowers	Skin care, stress relief, insomnia

Oatmeal

A HEALTHY BEGINNING

A bowl of oatmeal is one of the healthiest ways to start the day. Oats are filled with substances that are good for the circulatory and digestive systems. A scrub of oatmeal is one of the healthiest ways to care for your skin. Natural healers promote oats to help soothe the skin from skin ailments including itchiness, dryness, oiliness, eczema, dermatitis, bug bites, and poison ivy.

Oats soothe skin inflammation with a group of compounds called avenanthramides, which block the release of inflammatory compounds and histamines to reduce redness and itching. Oats also have antiviral and antifungal properties, which makes them useful in fighting the itch from chicken pox, shingles, and ringworm.

▶ OBTAINING AND USING

Oatmeal in many forms is readily available in any grocery store. It can be found in soaps, shampoos, ointments, and lotions. In the skin care aisle, you can find already prepared finely ground colloidal oatmeal (like Aveeno) available for purchase.

Bath: Put 1 cup oatmeal into a blender and process until finely ground. Pour the ground oatmeal into a tub of warm (not hot) water and soak for 15 minutes to relieve itching.

Paste: Grind up 4 cups oatmeal into a fine powder. Mix with 1/2 cup baking soda or cornstarch. Add 1/2 cup water to make a paste. Apply to affected area and let dry for 30 to 60 minutes. Rinse with cool water.

Common Name	Scientific Name	Parts Used	Therapeutic Uses
Oatmeal	*Avena sativa*	Leaves, flowers, fruits	Anti-itch treatment, dermatitis, psoriasis

Rosemary

SQUEAKY-CLEAN SKIN

Savory-smelling rosemary is a true herbal medicine multitasker. When applied to the skin, rosemary essential oil has been shown to exhibit antibacterial, antifungal, antiparasitic, and mild analgesic properties. It also is used topically to treat muscle pain and arthritis and to improve circulation; Germany's Commission E, which examines the safety and efficacy of herbs, has approved rosemary's use for these conditions.

PRECAUTIONS

A staple in cooking, rosemary leaves are safe to eat. However, rosemary essential oil is not harmless. Ingesting rosemary essential oil can cause seizures and can be toxic to the liver and heart. Use only under the guidance of a health care professional. Using rosemary as a seasoning during pregnancy is fine, but medicinal doses are not recommended.

Fragrant rosemary can be used in cooking as well as herbal medicine.

▶ OBTAINING AND USING

The best way to obtain fresh rosemary is simply to buy a plant at any gardening center. It is produced commercially in Spain, Portugal, and France, all countries of its natural range.

Creams, ointments, and salves: Many topical products contain various concentrations of rosemary's essential oil for skin conditions, such as minor bacterial or fungal infections. Apply daily to skin, joints, or muscles, as per manufacturer's directions.

Essential oil: The essential oil is used in aromatherapy to enhance mental focus. To apply the oil topically, mix 10 drops in 1 ounce carrier oil (olive, jojoba, almond, or apricot).

Tea: Add 1 to 2 teaspoons dried rosemary leaves to 1 cup hot water. Cover for 10 minutes, then strain. Drink 1 to 3 cups a day.

Capsules: Generally, take 500 to 1,000 mg once or twice daily; follow product instructions.

Common Name	Scientific Name	Parts Used	Therapeutic Uses
Rosemary	*Rosmarinus officinalis*	Leaves	Antiseptic, topical antioxidant, antibacterial

Tea Tree

NATURAL WONDER FROM DOWN UNDER

Tea tree essential oil has strong antibacterial and antifungal properties. It is used primarily to prevent and treat skin infections. Practitioners recommend it for acne, boils, warts, athlete's foot, ringworm, toenail fungus, dandruff, head lice, vaginal yeast infections, periodontal disease, eczema, psoriasis, and more.

Tea tree oil may be effective against antibiotic-resistant strains of bacteria, including methicillin-resistant *Staphylococcus aureus* (MRSA), and the herpes virus, though more research is needed to confirm this.

▶ OBTAINING AND USING

Tea tree is grown commercially on plantations in

The slender leaves of the tea tree are the source of tea tree oil.

> **RECIPE FOR HEALTH**
>
> **ATHLETE'S FOOT OINTMENT**
> Combine 1 drop lavender oil, 2 drops tea tree oil, and 1 teaspoon olive oil. Stir gently. Using a cotton swab, apply to infected areas of the foot several times daily. To prevent slipping, it may be helpful to cover with clean cotton socks. This natural fungicide can be applied to infections under the nails as well.

Australia and is a common ingredient in many creams, ointments, soaps, shampoos—and even toothpastes. In the United States, tea tree oil is available in most health food stores.

Cream or gel: Preparations of 5 percent tea tree oil control acne as well as a commonly used medication, benzoyl peroxide, and possibly with fewer side effects.

▶ PRECAUTIONS

Tea tree oil is a concentrate and should never be used undiluted or near sensitive areas such as eyes, nose, mouth, or genitals without guidance. Tea tree oil should never be taken internally; it can be toxic if ingested. Allergic reactions and contact dermatitis have also been documented. If redness, itching, or oozing develops after the topical application of tea tree oil, use should be discontinued and a health care provider consulted.

Common Name	Scientific Name	Parts Used	Therapeutic Uses
Tea tree	*Melaleuca alternifolia*	Leaves	Antifungal, antibacterial, gingivitis, dandruff

Witch Hazel

A NATURAL ASTRINGENT

Household first aid kits have long held distilled witch hazel water, one of the few widely available commercial medicines made from a wild native plant. The reason? Tannins in the leaves, bark, and twigs of witch hazel help heal a variety of skin conditions.

Various preparations of witch hazel are used topically to stop bleeding from minor cuts and abrasions; calm inflamed mucous membranes and skin, such as with eczema; and decrease the size and symptoms associated with varicose veins and hemorrhoids.

▶ OBTAINING AND USING

Witch hazel water can be found at any drugstore.

Extract: Many different forms of witch hazel begin with a distillation of the leaves, bark, and/or twigs. This liquid is added to ointment or creams and then applied to the skin.

Witch hazel's crinkly blossoms bloom in the late fall through early winter.

Liquid: Witch hazel water is made by soaking plant parts in water and distilling the mixture. The tinctures and other preparations commonly used by herbal medicine practitioners are usually stronger than distilled witch hazel water.

▶ PRECAUTIONS

Although there are witch hazel preparations that can be consumed orally, there is some concern about ingesting the tannin compounds in any appreciable quantity; they can cause stomach troubles and kidney or liver damage, or interfere with the absorption of vitamins and minerals. Common witch hazel from the drugstore is not safe to drink.

GOOD TO KNOW

1744   American doctor C. Colden wrote of "blindness" cured with a witch hazel decoction.

1846   T. Pond marketed a witch hazel patent medicine, Pond's Golden Treasure.

1882   A fluid extract of witch hazel was added to the *United States Pharmacopeia* (deleted 1914).

1915   Poet Robert Frost lamented the withering of witch hazel blossoms in "Reluctance."

Common Name	Scientific Names	Parts Used	Therapeutic Uses
Witch hazel	*Hamamelis virginiana, H. vernalis*	Leaves, bark, twigs	Antiseptic, minor cuts, hemorrhoids

Yarrow

A CLASSIC WOUND HEALER

Yarrow's genus name, *Achillea,* comes from Achilles, the Greek hero who used it to stanch the bleeding wounds of his soldiers. Yarrow flowers contain tannins that act as astringents, plus other compounds that slow the flow of blood. Yarrow contains more than 120 compounds in all, including azulene, an effective anti-inflammatory and fever reducer. Yarrow is also reported to improve digestion, balance hormones, and relax smooth muscle in the intestine and uterus, which can relieve stomach and menstrual cramps.

PRECAUTIONS

Yarrow has some dangerous potential interactions with other medications. Those taking blood-thinning medications (that is, anticoagulant and antiplatelet drugs) should not take yarrow, large amounts of which may increase the chances of bruising and bleeding. Lithium and yarrow are also a dangerous combination; check with your health care provider about potential problems if taking lithium.

Yarrow (Achillea millefolium)

▶ HISTORY

Yarrow has long been an essential part of battlefield medicine. Since the time of ancient Greece and Rome through the Middle Ages, soldiers would rub yarrow into their wounds and injuries. Even soldiers in the Civil War carried yarrow, called "soldier's woundwort," for the same reason.

▶ OBTAINING AND USING

The flowers, leaves, and stems of yarrow plants are used as medicine. Yarrow is available as a dried or fresh herb, in capsules or tablets, tinctures, and liquid extracts. Women who are pregnant or breast-feeding should not take yarrow orally.

Tea: Steep 1 tablespoon dried yarrow flowers in 1 cup hot water. Strain and drink a cup a day.

Extract: Take 1 to 4 ml, 3 times a day.

Common Name	Scientific Name	Parts Used	Therapeutic Uses
Yarrow	*Achillea millefolium*	Flowering tops, leaves, stems	Wound care

Lavender salt scrubs relax the mind as they polish the skin.

DO IT YOURSELF
Scrub-a-Dub-Dub

Exfoliating dead skin cells through body scrubs improves the skin's appearance, stimulates circulation, and makes it easier for natural oils and other skin-nurturing substances to be absorbed.

To use a body scrub, massage with your fingers in small, circular motions. Continue until you've covered your entire body. Rinse and shower as usual. A weekly scrub should do the trick without damage.

Something Sweet. Ordinary table sugar is an effective exfoliant: inexpensive, odorless, and easily blended with a variety of oils. Combine 1/2 cup white sugar with enough almond oil to completely moisten. Add a squeeze of fresh lemon juice and stir well to make sure the sugar is saturated with the oil and juice.

Go Nuts. Ground almonds and oatmeal are also good body scrub bases. Combine 2/3 cup coarsely chopped almonds, 1/3 cup regular (not quick) oatmeal, and 1/2 teaspoon dried sage or rosemary in a food processor. Pulse until the mixture resembles medium-coarse meal. Add almond oil to make a thick but spreadable paste.

ROSEMARY SALT SCRUB

Blend 1/2 cup grape seed or almond oil, 1/4 cup avocado or olive oil, the contents of 1 vitamin E capsule, and 10 to 15 drops rosemary oil in a small bowl. Add 1 cup fine-grain sea salt, and mix well. Store in a container with an airtight lid.

CHAPTER SEVEN

MEN'S HEALTH

NATURAL REMEDIES FOR HIM

The different anatomies of men and women often require different medical treatments. For instance, the urinary system in both men and women is essentially the same in that it consists of the kidneys, ureters, bladder, and urethra. What is very different is that men have a structure, the prostate gland, which encircles the neck of the bladder like a doughnut precisely at the point where it joins the urethra. As men age, the prostate typically enlarges, which can lead to serious bladder and kidney problems. Other aging changes that occur in the male reproductive system include decreases in sperm production and testosterone levels, changes in the tissues that form the testes and the tubes and ducts, and erectile dysfunction.

The natural remedies highlighted on the following pages have been selected among many as having a long history of use in treating male health-related problems or those that commonly affect the urinary tract, both in men and women.

Opposite: Exercise is one part of a healthy lifestyle.
Above: Pomegranate seeds (*Punica granatum*)

Saw Palmetto

PROSTATE'S POWERFUL PALM

Native to the southeastern United States, saw palmetto is a low-growing palm with distinctive fan-shaped leaves. Vast, unbroken tracts of saw palmetto once covered hundreds of miles of coastal land in Florida, Georgia, and other parts of southeastern North America. The dark purple fruits of saw palmetto—about the size and shape of olives—were an indispensable dietary staple among Native American tribes for perhaps as long as 12,000 years before Europeans set foot in this part of the world.

In modern herbal medicine, saw palmetto is primarily used to treat benign prostatic hyperplasia (BPH), an enlargement of the prostate gland. It is used by two million men in the United States alone. Some herbal practitioners also recommend saw palmetto for chronic pelvic pain syndrome (CPPS) in men, inflammation of the urethra, bladder disorders, and gallbladder problems.

▶ **HISTORY**

The Seminole and other tribes in the southeastern United States had a long tradition of using saw palmetto for urinary complaints, digestive problems,

Extracts from saw palmetto berries are used to treat prostate problems.

and dysentery, and as an aphrodisiac, an expectorant, an antiseptic, and a tonic to improve general health. When European settlers arrived, they added saw palmetto to their diet and fed the fruits to their livestock. They observed the native tribes using saw palmetto, particularly as a remedy for urinary tract complaints. By the late 1800s, the plant had found its way into conventional medicine in the United States.

Early 20th-century conventional and American Eclectic physicians recommended saw palmetto for a variety of health problems. In particular, preparations of the fruits were given to help resolve urinary tract infections, to alleviate symptoms of enlarged prostate, and to boost libido. Although interest in herbs of all kinds had faded in the United States by the 1950s, saw palmetto use in Europe steadily increased. European companies were among the first to produce standardized extracts of saw palmetto fruit.

▶ OBTAINING AND USING

Saw palmetto is found in pine scrub, dunes, and hummocks, often in dense colonies in the southeastern United States. Given its common and abundant occurrence in Florida, it is rarely cultivated. Millions of pounds of saw palmetto berries are harvested each year mostly in Florida, but also in southern Georgia and adjacent Alabama. It may take 1 to 2 months of using saw palmetto to begin to experience the full benefits of the herb.

Extract: Studies have used a specific extract, standardized at 80 to 90 percent fatty acids and sterols—the compounds most effective for BPH symptoms—and dosed at 160 mg, twice daily.

Tincture: Take 1 to 2 ml, 3 times a day.

HOW TO HARVEST

Saw palmetto berries are typically gathered by hand from wild plants in southern Florida. Saw palmetto thickets, source of the majority of berries harvested for commercial trade, cover millions of Florida acres. Despite high heat and humidity, pickers wear long sleeves and leather gloves for protection against the razor-sharp spines edging the plants' leaf stalks. Eastern diamondback rattlesnakes rest in the shade of saw palmetto, and wasps build large nests in the center of the shrub, making berry harvest a daunting task. Freshly picked berries need to be dried before being shipped to extractors, mostly in Europe; extracts return to the United States for incorporation into products.

Capsules: Follow manufacturer's guidelines.

▶ PRECAUTIONS

Saw palmetto can cause mild stomach upset, constipation, diarrhea, headache, high blood pressure, and itching. In rare cases, saw palmetto can cause impotence or decreased sex drive. Due to its possible hormonal effects, saw palmetto is not recommended for those on hormone therapy, nor during pregnancy.

Common Name	Scientific Name	Parts Used	Therapeutic Use
Saw palmetto	*Serenoa repens*	Fruits	Benign prostatic hyperplasia (BPH)

Broccoli

SUPER FOOD FOR SUPER HEALTH

An apple a day might keep the doctor away, but a cup of broccoli could do so much more. One cup of broccoli contains 165 percent of the daily value of vitamin C! It's also unusually rich in vitamin A, vitamin K, folate (a water-soluble B-group vitamin), and a variety of antioxidants. But beware: Too much broccoli (or kale and related foods) can affect the absorption of iodine and lead to hypothyroidism.

Broccoli is a great addition to anyone's diet, but there are specific health benefits for men. Broccoli's high vitamin A, vitamin C, and folic acid content all encourage increased sperm count in men suffering from infertility.

Broccoli (*Brassica oleracea*)

▶ OBTAINING AND USING

First cultivated in Italy, broccoli's benefits are best absorbed as part of your regular diet. Both fresh and frozen broccoli can be purchased at any grocery store.

Selecting: Look for firm florets with a purple, dark green, or bluish color, which indicates a higher beta-carotene and vitamin C content.

Storing: Keep uncooked broccoli unwashed and wrapped in paper towels in the crisper drawer; alternatively, cut off about a half inch from the bottom of each main stalk and stand upright in a small bowl or glass with enough water to cover the cut stem.

Cooking: Fresh broccoli cooks quickly. Just steam or sauté for 5 minutes. Don't overcook, or some of the valuable nutrients will be lost.

GOOD TO KNOW

- The sulfur compounds in cruciferous veggies like broccoli also support healthy liver function and metabolism.

- Try sipping peppermint tea after eating a meal that includes broccoli, as it sometimes causes intestinal gas.

- In 1767, Thomas Jefferson was the first to cultivate broccoli in America.

- Half a cup of broccoli contains only 22 calories.

Common Name	Scientific Name	Parts Used	Therapeutic Uses
Broccoli	*Brassica oleracea*	Stems, florets	Overall wellness, antioxidant, fertility

Horny Goat Weed

TRUTH IN ADVERTISING

A plant with a long history of use in Chinese medicine, horny goat weed is a popular remedy for men's health issues. It has been used medicinally for more than 2,000 years. It was first described in ancient classical medicinal texts of China, where it still grows wild today. The colorful name is said to come from folk observations that goats that grazed on the herb became unusually sexually active. Practitioners of Chinese medicine typically use horny goat weed in combination with other herbs to treat male sexual dysfunction, prostate problems, urinary

Horny goat weed is called *yin yang huo* in Chinese medicine.

PRECAUTIONS

More research on horny goat weed is being conducted because the exact safety of the herb is unknown. Safety in people with severe liver or kidney disease has not been established. Long-term use of some forms of horny goat weed might cause dizziness, vomiting, dry mouth, thirst, and nosebleed. Large dosages might cause spasms and severe breathing problems.

tract issues, and other issues associated with aging.

The leaves of horny goat weed, a species of *Epimedium,* are used in medical applications. The leaves contain a variety of flavonoids, polysaccharides, sterols, and an alkaloid called magnaflorine. But the plant's exact mechanism is unknown, although research is ongoing. One lab study found that a compound in horny goat weed improves libido and erectile dysfunction by blocking an enzyme that restricts blood flow.

▶ OBTAINING AND USING

Horny goat weed is sold in drugstores and health food stores in a variety of forms. It is often blended with other herbal remedies (most often maca root), so check the label for ingredients.

Capsules: Follow the manufacturer's instructions. Most scientific studies of horny goat weed relied on dosages of 6 to 15 g a day.

Common Name	Scientific Name	Parts Used	Therapeutic Uses
Horny goat weed	*Epimedium brevicornum*	Leaves	Sexual health, prostate health, urinary tract health

Juniper

BETTER HEALTH BERRIES

Juniper (*Juniperus communis*)

Juniper is used to treat urinary tract infections and to stimulate urine production by the kidneys (but not to treat kidney infection). Juniper is also recommended, externally and internally, for relieving swelling, the pain of rheumatoid arthritis and other joint pain, muscle pain, and tendonitis. Topically, the herb's essential oil has been used in treating respiratory infections, congestion, and coughs and for stubborn skin conditions, including psoriasis.

▶ OBTAINING AND USING

Much of the world's supply of juniper berries is harvested in eastern Europe. Extracts, oils, and capsules are widely available commercially.

Extract: Juniper berry extract is an alcohol-based liquid that is extracted from the ripe fruits; dosage is typically 1 to 4 ml, 3 times daily.

Essential oil: Do not take the essential oil orally. To apply to the skin, mix 10 drops essential oil in 1 ounce carrier oil.

Capsules: Take 425 to 850 mg, 3 times a day; juniper is often taken in combination with other herbs for urinary health.

▶ PRECAUTIONS

Check with a health care provider before using juniper berries. Concerns have been reported with the ingestion of juniper extracts acting as an abortifacient in animals; oral use of these oils should be avoided during pregnancy. Juniper oils or extracts should not be used by anyone with a kidney infection or kidney disease.

Common Name	Scientific Name	Parts Used	Therapeutic Uses
Juniper	*Juniperus communis*	Cones (berries)	Urinary tract infections, bronchitis

Pomegranate

A BIG JUICY CURE

Compared with other common fruit juices, pomegranate is one of the richest in antioxidant activity—with roughly three times that of red wine and green tea! Animal studies show that pomegranate juice and pomegranate flower extract offer strong protection against the progression of atherosclerosis. Human studies demonstrate a modest effect on blood pressure and inflammation reduction—reasons for adding pomegranate to a heart-healthy-foods list.

Rich in antioxidants, pomegranate juice is a healthful drink, high in vitamin C, in its unsweetened form. The juice may help prevent or slow the progression

of some cancers, including prostate cancer. It has been shown to lower blood pressure, improve blood flow to the heart, and inhibit plaque formation in arteries, but more research is needed.

▶ OBTAINING AND USING

This luscious fruit has been used as food and medicine for at least 4 millennia. Pomegranate grows in warmer regions; it survives light frosts of short duration but generally requires a long, hot summer for fruit ripening. Even in areas where the growing season is not long enough to produce fruit, the beauty of the flowers alone makes it worth the effort as a container plant. Large-scale production occurs in California, India, Australia, and elsewhere.

Juice: Drink 8 ounces of juice a day (the typical amount used in research studies).

Capsules: Generally, take 2 to 3 g powdered pomegranate daily.

The juice of pomegranate seeds is a rich source of antioxidants.

Common Name	Scientific Name	Parts Used	Therapeutic Uses
Pomegranate	*Punica granatum*	Fruits, seeds	Prostate health, heart health

Pygeum
BEST BARK AROUND

The African cherry, or pygeum, tree grows in tropical mountain forests in Africa and Madagascar. The tree bark has been used to treat many ailments, including problems with the urinary tract. In the United States today, pygeum is used as a treatment for enlarged prostate, or benign prostate hyperplasia (BPH). Pygeum bark is also used to help those who suffer with excessive nighttime urination, painful urination, or the sensation of a full bladder, common symptoms of BPH.

▶ HISTORY
In Africa, pygeum bark has a long history as a pain-killer and anti-inflammatory. Traditionally, the bark is ground to a powder and drunk as a tea to treat

Pygeum is a relative of the cherry tree.

malaria, fever, stomach and intestinal disorders, lung ailments, kidney disease, menstrual complaints, infertility, and even mental illness.

▶ OBTAINING AND USING
Pygeum standardized extracts are available at most drug and health food stores. Pygeum is over-harvested in the wild, and consumers should take care to buy it from sustainable sources.

Extract: Pygeum bark extracts are usually dosed at 100 mg daily. Taking 100 mg daily in a standardized extract may have benefits for several symptoms associated with BPH.

▶ PRECAUTIONS
Nausea, diarrhea, constipation, stomach upset, headache, and dizziness have been reported when taking pygeum. Safety in pregnancy and lactation is not known.

Common Name	Scientific Name	Parts Used	Therapeutic Use
Pygeum	*Prunus africana*	Bark	Benign prostatic hyperplasia (BPH)

Spinach

LEAN, GREEN HEALTH MACHINE

Popeye the Sailor Man ate a lot of spinach to build up his muscles. Science shows, however, that spinach is good for a lot more than that. To nourish the bones, spinach is rich in calcium and vitamin K, which keeps bones strong and dense.

Spinach also contains phosphorus, potassium, zinc, and selenium. This strong combination may give spinach the power to protect the liver, ward off Alzheimer's disease, and prevent prostate and colon cancers.

▶ OBTAINING AND USING

Spinach grows well in temperate climates. Today, the United States and the Netherlands are among the largest commercial producers.

Selecting: Fresh spinach is preferable to frozen or canned. When buying at the store, look for leaves that are bright green and fully alive (not wilted).

Vibrant green spinach leaves contain more vitamin C than pale ones.

Studies have shown that these greener leaves have more vitamin C. Having 1 cup cooked spinach 4 times a week should help you realize the benefits of this vegetable.

▶ PRECAUTIONS

Spinach contains oxalic acid, which reduces how much calcium and iron your body will absorb. To thwart this action, pair spinach with vitamin C–rich foods like tomatoes and citrus fruit. You can also boil spinach for about 1 minute to reduce the oxalic acid content.

RECIPE FOR HEALTH

GREEN EGGS (HAM OPTIONAL)
In a small bowl, mix 2 eggs, 2 tablespoons milk, and a pinch of salt with a fork. Cook the egg mixture in a nonstick skillet. Add about 1/2 cup finely chopped fresh spinach to scrambled eggs, about 30 seconds before the eggs are completely set. (The eggs don't actually turn green—they just look beautiful.)

Common Name	Scientific Name	Parts Used	Therapeutic Uses
Spinach	*Spinacia oleracea*	Leaves	Prostate health, bone health

Stinging Nettle

FIGHTING PAIN WITH PAIN

Scientists believe stinging nettle lowers levels of certain inflammatory chemicals in the body, and possibly interferes with pain signals transmission. Stinging nettle's unique ability to fight pain with pain has made it a valuable addition to herbal medicine.

Modern herbal practitioners recommend nettle preparations as an antihistamine and to treat rheumatism; joint pain from osteoarthritis; and strains, sprains, and tendonitis. The root of the stinging nettle plant is widely used in Europe to treat symptoms of early-stage benign prostatic hyperplasia (BPH).

▶ OBTAINING AND USING

Dried nettles can be purchased in capsules as well as standardized extracts.

Even the leaves on stinging nettle plants have needle-sharp bristles.

> **RECIPE FOR HEALTH**
>
> **STINGING NETTLE PESTO**
> Blanch 6 cups fresh nettle leaves in boiling water for 1 minute to deactivate the "sting." Drain, pat dry, and roughly chop. Combine the leaves, 1/3 cup olive oil, 1/2 cup grated Parmesan cheese, 1/3 cup pine nuts or walnuts, 3 cloves minced garlic, 1/2 teaspoon salt, and 1/8 teaspoon pepper in a food processor and blend until smooth.

Decoction: Boil 5 g chopped, dried root in 2 cups water for 10 minutes. Strain, cool, and consume throughout the day.

Capsules: Dried, powdered root extracts in capsule form can be taken in doses of 300 to 800 mg daily, depending on the formulation.

Tincture: Use 1 to 3 teaspoons daily of an alcohol-based liquid extract of the root.

Extract: Some may combine stinging nettle root and saw palmetto berries; others contain pumpkin seed oil. Follow manufacturer's dosage guidelines.

▶ PRECAUTIONS

Side effects may include upset stomach, rash, and impotence. Those taking medicines for diabetes, high blood pressure, anxiety, or insomnia should exercise caution with stinging nettle preparations because interactions are possible.

Common Name	Scientific Name	Parts Used	Therapeutic Uses
Stinging nettle	*Urtica dioica*	Leaves, roots	Benign prostatic hyperplasia (BPH), allergies

Tomato

THE SECRET OF LYCOPENE

Tomato *(Lycopersicon esculentum)*

Tomatoes contain a compound called lycopene—known to be important for prostate health. Lycopene is a carotenoid, an antioxidant found in fruits and vegetables. Lycopene may act in several different ways to inhibit the growth of cancer cells and affect inflammation or immune system function. Tomatoes also contain vitamin C and other carotenoids that make it a healthful food beneficial for many medical conditions.

Research suggests that consuming tomatoes and tomato products—and hence lycopene—lowers risk for developing prostate cancer. The medicinal use of lycopene is still being debated and defined. The varied effects of lycopene are also of interest to researchers for the treatment or prevention of liver, breast, pancreatic, lung, and gastric cancers.

▶ OBTAINING AND USING

Tomatoes, and in particular cooked tomato products, provide lycopene and other nutrients relevant to prostate cancer prevention. One estimate is that 10 servings a week of cooked tomatoes provide the best benefit for prostate cancer prevention. In addition, capsules containing 5 to 15 mg lycopene can be taken once a day.

▶ PRECAUTIONS

Some antioxidants are of concern for people undergoing chemotherapy or radiation therapy. Simply eating tomatoes during these treatments is safe, but check with a health care provider before adding lycopene to any cancer treatment protocol.

Common Name	Scientific Name	Parts Used	Therapeutic Uses
Tomato	*Lycopersicon esculentum*	Fruit	Prostate health

Uva Ursi

A FIGHTING ANTI-INFLAMMATORY

Uva ursi leaves have known astringent and antibacterial properties, making them effective in reducing inflammation and fighting infection. Uva ursi is used primarily to treat inflammations of the urinary tract, including chronic cases that have become resistant to conventional antibiotics. In Germany, the leaf is available as a standardized medicinal tea. Externally, preparations of uva ursi are used to bathe cuts and scrapes, to treat cold sores, and to ease back pain.

PRECAUTIONS

Uva ursi contains a chemical, hydroquinone, that can damage the liver. Uva ursi should be taken for no longer than 5 to 10 days under a health care provider's supervision. Uva ursi is not recommended for children, pregnant women, lactating mothers, or those with renal failure. The tannins in uva ursi can cause stomach upset, nausea, vomiting, and constipation. It should not be taken with lithium.

Uva ursi's scarlet berries draw attention to the otherwise humble plant.

▶ OBTAINING AND USING

Uva ursi is found growing among coastal dunes and on inhospitable mountaintops at elevations above 7,000 feet, and can remain hardy at temperatures as low as minus 50°F (-45.6°C). Herbalists in its North American range harvest uva ursi on a small scale. Some commercial harvesting occurs in Canada. But the vast majority of the world's supply of uva ursi comes from the wild-harvesting that takes place in the mountains and valleys of eastern Europe. The dried leaves and tinctures are sold in most health food stores.

Tea: Generally, a common dose of uva ursi dried leaf is 1 teaspoon dried herb steeped in 1 cup boiling water. The tea can be taken 3 to 4 times daily.

Capsules: Standardized extracts of 700 to 1,000 mg can be taken 3 times daily.

Tincture: Generally, take 5 ml (1 teaspoon), 3 times a day.

Common Name	Scientific Name	Parts Used	Therapeutic Use
Uva ursi	*Arctostaphylos uva-ursi*	Leaves	Urinary tract infections

DO IT YOURSELF
Clean, Close Shave

Homemade shaving solutions can offer a clean, close shave without the skin irritation and dryness.

Plant Oils. Just use oil. Pure plant oils, such as olive, almond, or grape seed oil, act as natural lubricants and so help a razor glide easily over skin. You don't need to use much. Because the oil is a natural moisturizer, it will leave skin smooth, supple, and protected.

Infused Oil. Essential oils blended with plant oil can enhance a shave, making it relaxing or invigorating. To create a skin-soothing oil for shaving, add 1 or 2 drops chamomile essential oil to 1/2 cup plant oil. Or make a refreshing oil by adding a few drops eucalyptus essential oil to the same amount of oil. Use as previously advised.

Lather Up! For those who prefer the traditional feel of lathering up, try using all-natural castile soap in liquid or bar form. It produces a rich, creamy lather naturally. Follow with a skin-softening natural aftershave lotion.

**RECIPE FOR HEALTH:
HOMEMADE AFTERSHAVE**

In a glass jar with a tight-fitting lid, combine:

1 cup real witch hazel extract
1/2 cup high-proof vodka, rum, or brandy
1 to 2 tablespoons vegetable glycerin
10 to 20 drops each peppermint and eucalyptus essential oil

Shake well to blend. To use, pat a little of the mixture onto just shaved skin. The lotion keeps indefinitely.

CHAPTER EIGHT

WOMEN'S HEALTH

NATURAL REMEDIES FOR HER

Women and men share many body systems, and therefore many similar health problems. But women also have their own health issues, most involving the reproductive system. Its major organs consist of the ovaries, which produce egg cells and various hormones; the uterus, a muscular-walled structure characterized by an extensive blood vessel system; and the oviducts, or fallopian tubes, which essentially connect the ovaries to the uterus and provide a passageway down which eggs can move. Women's lives are also governed, and their health often affected, by a number of physiological conditions and events. These include the menstrual cycle, pregnancy, and menopause.

For thousands of years, herbal medicines were the only way to maintain the health of the female reproductive system through all these stages. Natural remedies were also the primary way available to treat problems associated with the reproductive system. Today, many women still rely on herbal medicine to help alleviate some of these problems.

Opposite: Natural remedies can help restore balance to the body.
Above: Chaste tree *(Vitex agnus-castus)*

Cranberry

A TART TREATMENT

Ruby red and exceedingly tart, the American cranberry is native to the swamps and bogs of northeastern North America. In herbal and conventional medicine today, cranberry is widely used to prevent—not treat—urinary tract infections. Originally it was thought that cranberry prevented these infections by acidifying urine; however, scientists have shown that compounds known as proanthocyanidins prevent harmful bacteria such as *Escherichia coli* from adhering to the cells that line the bladder and urethra. This is good news given that *E. coli* is responsible for 90 percent of urinary tract infections.

Herbal practitioners also recommend it for kidney and bladder stones, incontinence, and prostate problems for men. It also may help prevent bacteria-induced stomach ulcers, lower LDL ("bad") cholesterol in the blood, and, in the lab, inhibit growth of some types of cancer cells.

▶ HISTORY

Cranberries were an important food for Native Americans. They ate the berries cooked and sweetened

Tart cranberries are loaded with bacteria-fighting substances.

with maple syrup or honey and as an ingredient in pemmican, a nutritious, high-calorie mixture of dried venison, fat, and dried fruit that was an essential winter staple.

The Indians also employed cranberry medicinally; it was applied as a poultice for cuts and abrasions and arrow wounds, and as a cure for indigestion, kidney diseases, and lung ailments. Native Americans introduced the cranberry to European colonists, who quickly adopted it as both food and medicine. It became a remedy for digestive problems, gallbladder attacks, blood disorders, and kidney stones. In the same way that British sailors used limes, New England sailors and whalers ate cranberries while at sea to prevent scurvy.

▶ OBTAINING AND USING

Cranberry can still be found growing wild in bog habitats of its native range, which extends from eastern Canada south to the mountains of Georgia and west as far as Minnesota. Most of the cranberries that now find their way into foods and drinks—and grace millions of Thanksgiving tables—are cultivated on large commercial farms.

The primary cranberry fruit production states are Wisconsin, Massachusetts, Oregon, New Jersey, and Washington. Cranberries can be bought fresh at supermarkets in season or frozen. Cranberry juice is also widely available, as are cranberry extracts.

Juice: Drinking cranberry juice is an easy and tasty way to prevent urinary tract infections.

Extract: Cranberry extract in tablet form has been shown to be as effective, better tolerated, less expensive, and lower in calories when compared with the juice. The dose of concentrated juice extract is 300 to 500 mg, taken twice a day.

HOW TO HARVEST

In the United States and Canada, cranberry plants grow in sandy fields called bogs. Because cranberry fruits contain pockets of air, they float in water. As a result, "wet harvesting" is the most common way to gather ripe cranberries. In late autumn, the bogs are flooded with water, and harvesters use water reels, machines that agitate the water, to help remove the berries from the plants. As berries float to the surface, harvesters use rake-like "brooms" to corral the berries in a corner of the bog. Cranberries ride a conveyor belt out of the bog. Trucks will carry the berries to cleaning facilities.

▶ PRECAUTIONS

Given the widespread use of cranberry by the general public, it is safe to say that there are no adverse effects associated with cranberry use. It is safe during pregnancy and lactation and for children. Although several case reports have indicated a concern for a potential interaction between cranberry juice and warfarin, used to prevent blood clots, human studies have documented no adverse interactions.

Common Name	Scientific Name	Parts Used	Therapeutic Use
Cranberry	*Vaccinium macrocarpon*	Fruit	Bladder health

Black Cohosh

CALMING ROOTS

Black cohosh has become very popular for treating menstrual cramps, premenstrual discomfort, and menopausal symptoms. Early studies suggested that black cohosh acts like a natural estrogen, or phytoestrogen, but newer research has found no hormonal effects of black cohosh in menopausal women. In the United States, interest in black cohosh is on the rise. Herbal practitioners recommend it for menopause symptoms, as well as irritability, mood swings, and anxiety. It may be an effective alternative for women who cannot or will not take hormone replacement therapy.

▶ OBTAINING AND USING

Black cohosh is widely available in stores. Much of today's commercial supply now grows in Europe and China.

Black cohosh (*Actaea racemosa*)

RECIPE FOR HEALTH

MENOPAUSE TINCTURE
This tincture can be used during the menopausal transition. Take 5 ml (1 teaspoon) morning and night. Mix 1/2 ounce black cohosh rhizome, 1/2 ounce shatavari, and 1/2 ounce chaste tree fruit in a coffee grinder. Grind herbs and place in a quart jar. Pour 6 ounces vodka over herbs, stir well, and close tightly. Let sit for 14 days, and then strain liquid. Store in a dark glass jar.

Tea: Simmer 2 teaspoons chopped root and rhizome in 2 cups water for 10 minutes. Strain. Drink 1/4 cup, 2 to 3 times a day.

Capsules: Take 40 to 200 mg dried rhizome daily, in divided doses.

Tincture: Generally, take 1 to 2 ml, 3 times a day.

Standardized extract: Take 20 to 40 mg black cohosh extract twice daily. Products are often standardized to provide 1 to 2 mg of 27-deoxyactein.

▶ PRECAUTIONS

Except for minor gastrointestinal upset, clinical trials have shown black cohosh to be free of side effects. A few reports have suggested that black cohosh may, in rare cases, cause damage to the liver, so monitor carefully for signs of liver damage if using. Do not take it during pregnancy, and consult a physician before taking it while breast-feeding.

Common Name	Scientific Name	Parts Used	Therapeutic Uses
Black cohosh	*Actaea racemosa*	Roots, rhizomes	Menopause, premenstrual syndrome, menstrual cramps

Black Haw

CRAMP-RELIEVING BARK

Black haw eases menstrual pain and cramps. It is used to treat menopausal symptoms and calm uterine muscles, particularly in cases where muscle spasms might lead to miscarriage. Animal studies have confirmed that compounds in the bark of the root and stems relax the uterus, trachea, and small intestine by interacting with beta-adrenergic receptors in the smooth muscles—the same mechanism that many prescription drugs work to relax these tissues.

▶ OBTAINING AND USING

The branch and trunk bark of black haw are the parts used in herbal medicine. The herb is sold dried and in capsule, extract, and tincture forms.

Tea: Simmer 2 teaspoons dried root or stem bark in 1 cup water for 5 to 7 minutes. Strain. Drink 1/4 cup every 2 to 3 hours, to 2 cups daily.

Capsules: Typically, 1,000 mg is taken 3 times a day.

Black haw bark contains compounds that relax the muscles of the uterus.

Tincture: Take 5 to 10 ml of the tincture 3 times a day.

▶ PRECAUTIONS

No adverse effects from the use of black haw are reported in medical literature. Black haw may contain small amounts of salicin, a compound related to aspirin. Those allergic to aspirin could theoretically be allergic to black haw, though this has not been reported. Black haw should not be used during pregnancy except under the direction of a health care professional.

Common Name	Scientific Name	Parts Used	Therapeutic Uses
Black haw	*Viburnum prunifolium*	Root and stem bark	Menstrual cramps, muscle cramps

Chaste Tree

TREE OF LIFE

When chaste tree fruits ripen, they turn dark and resemble peppercorns.

Chaste tree (also called vitex) preparations are used to manage menstrual disorders, including premenstrual syndrome (PMS). Women also take the herb to relieve some of the symptoms of menopause, such as hot flashes. Chaste tree is sometimes recommended for women having difficulty conceiving. Chaste tree extracts, used daily for at least three months, have been shown to restore progesterone levels, which may improve female fertility. However, more investigation needs to be done before recommendations can be made.

▶ OBTAINING AND USING

Commercial production of chaste tree occurs in Italy and in China. Extracts, teas, tinctures, and capsules are all available.

Tea: Steep 1/2 teaspoon dried chaste tree fruit in 1 cup hot water for 5 to 7 minutes. Strain. Drink 1 cup each morning. Note: The tea is somewhat spicy and acrid in taste.

Capsules: Take 250 to 500 mg dried chaste tree fruit once a day.

Tincture: Take 2 to 3 ml tincture each morning.

Standardized extract: Take 20 to 40 mg chaste tree extract once a day.

▶ PRECAUTIONS

Chaste tree appears to be extremely well tolerated in clinical trials. Although no adverse effects have been reported in pregnancy, women should consult a health care provider before using chaste tree for infertility, and before discontinuing use during pregnancy.

Common Name	Scientific Name	Parts Used	Therapeutic Uses
Chaste tree	*Vitex agnus-castus*	Fruits	Premenstrual syndrome, breast tenderness

Dong Quai
THE FEMALE GINSENG

Dong quai root has been used for millennia as a medicine in China, Korea, and Japan. It is one of the most widely prescribed herbs in Chinese medicine, and is used—typically in combination with other herbs—primarily to treat women. For this reason, it is sometimes referred to as female ginseng. In the West, herbal practitioners recommend dong quai for women's reproductive problems, as well as premenstrual syndrome (PMS). Some women also take dong quai to relieve hot flashes and other symptoms of menopause.

Dong quai has been widely used in Chinese traditional medicine.

RECIPE FOR HEALTH

CHICKEN SOUP WITH DONG QUAI
Combine the following in a slow cooker: 1 pound skinless, boneless chicken breasts (hormone-free); 8 cups water or organic chicken broth; 1 medium onion, chopped; 2 carrots, chopped; 2 cloves garlic; 1/2 teaspoon thyme; 1 small root dong quai; 2 teaspoons salt; and 1 teaspoon pepper. Cook on low for 8 to 10 hours.

▶ OBTAINING AND USING
Dong quai grows at elevations well over a mile high. Since the roots are easily damaged if mishandled, they must be carefully dug out by hand and rinsed. If the roots become too wet, they will turn black on the outside and may rot.

Tea: Simmer 1 to 2 teaspoons root in 1 cup water for 5 to 7 minutes. Strain. Drink 1 cup, 2 to 3 times a day.

Capsules: Take 1 g, 2 to 3 times daily.

Tincture: Take 3 to 5 ml, 2 to 3 times daily.

▶ PRECAUTIONS
Those with bleeding disorders or who are taking anticoagulants should not use dong quai, as it may increase risk of bleeding. Use should be avoided during pregnancy. The psoralen in dong quai could, in theory, cause photosensitivity.

Common Name	Scientific Name	Parts Used	Therapeutic Uses
Dong quai	*Angelica sinensis*	Roots	Women's tonic, premenstrual syndrome, cramps

Motherwort

A NEW MOTHER'S LITTLE HELPER

Motherwort is traditionally given to new mothers to treat conditions related to childbirth. Herbalists use motherwort to regulate the menstrual cycle and to treat menstrual complaints. The herb may also help relieve nervousness, insomnia, heart palpitations, and rapid heart rate.

Motherwort contains a chemical called leonurine that has been shown to affect how the uterus contracts. One study found that the high dosages of leonurine made the uterus relax while low doses made it contract. These effects may explain why motherwort can be given both to women to provoke the onset of menstruation as well as to women who have just given birth.

Motherwort belongs to the same family as mint.

GOOD TO KNOW

- The ancient Greeks and Romans used motherwort to treat heart conditions.
- In eastern China, new mothers are given sugar as a gift, to counteract the bitter taste of motherwort syrup traditionally drunk after giving birth.
- Other common names for motherwort include: throw-wort, lion's ear, and lion's tail.
- Motherwort is a member of the mint family.

▶ OBTAINING AND USING

Although motherwort is indigenous to Europe, the plant grows all over the world in many different climates and settings: vacant lots, forests, open areas. Motherwort is also cultivated as a garden plant and is harvested during the summer.

Dried herb: Take 4.5 g daily.

▶ PRECAUTIONS

Motherwort has not been well studied, but side effects appear to be rare. It should not be used by pregnant women or women with a history of breast cancer, nor should it be used after childbirth without medical supervision. Nursing women and those with kidney or liver disease should also avoid motherwort. Also, do not combine motherwort with heart medications, as they might interact unpredictably.

Common Name	Scientific Name	Parts Used	Therapeutic Uses
Motherwort	*Leonurus cardiaca*	Leaves, seeds	Amenorrhea, heart health

Raspberry Leaf

BERRY GOOD HEALTH

Raspberry leaf tea has long been drunk to regulate menstrual cycles and ease menstrual cramps. It also has a long tradition of use during pregnancy. Today, herbalists recommend raspberry leaf preparations to strengthen, tone, and relax smooth muscles of the uterus and pelvis; shorten labor; and ease delivery. Raspberry tea may also help regulate menstrual cycles and decrease heavy menstrual flow.

▶ OBTAINING AND USING

Raspberry is easy to grow. It needs room to spread, although careful training in rows or along a fence will help keep it under control.

Tea: Steep 1 to 2 teaspoons dried raspberry leaves in 1 cup water for 5 minutes. Strain. Add honey and/or lemon as desired. Drink 1 cup 2 to 3 times a day. To extract the tannins to ease sore throat or diarrhea, the tea must be steeped for a longer period, 15 to 30 minutes. Generally, the dose is 1/3 cup taken 3 to 4 times a day as needed.

Raspberry leaves are prized as a pregnancy aid.

Capsules: Take 500 to 600 mg dried raspberry leaf, 2 to 4 times daily.

Tincture: Take 5 ml 2 times a day, or follow manufacturer's directions.

▶ PRECAUTIONS

Raspberry leaf appears to be quite safe, and no significant adverse effects were made note of in clinical studies published in medical literature. However, women should always check with a health care practitioner before using herbal remedies during pregnancy.

RECIPE FOR HEALTH

RASPBERRY BLISS TEA
Pour 4 cups boiling water over 6 teaspoons dried raspberry leaves and 2 teaspoons dried spearmint leaves. Steep for 5 to 7 minutes. Strain. Add 1/2 cup fruit juice—apple, grape, or raspberry. The tea will keep in the refrigerator for 3 to 4 days.

Common Name	Scientific Name	Parts Used	Therapeutic Uses
Raspberry leaf	*Rubus idaeus*	Leaves	Women's tonic, pregnancy tea

Shatavari

TANGLING ROOTS

Shatavari (*Asparagus racemosus*)

Shatavari grows throughout tropical and subtropical parts of India and in the Himalaya. Its name is Sanskrit for "plant of a hundred roots," which reflects shatavari's profusion of roots.

Ayurvedic practitioners commonly recommend shatavari to maintain the function of the female reproductive organs. The plant has recently become popular, as it is said to enhance fertility and is often used to normalize irregular menstrual cycles, especially when they are caused by stress or illness. One open study found that a formulation containing shatavari eased menstrual cramps, regulated uterine bleeding, and improved symptoms of premenstrual syndrome (PMS) in a small group of women. Shatavari, often in combination with other herbs, is also popular for relieving menopausal symptoms such as hot flashes, night sweats, and vaginal dryness.

▶ PRECAUTIONS

Shatavari appears safe and generally well tolerated if used appropriately. However, shatavari is not recommended for use during pregnancy.

▶ OBTAINING AND USING

In various parts of India, the root is wild-collected for use. Shatavari can be purchased in several forms, including dried root powder, capsules, and extracts.

Tea: Simmer 1 teaspoon dried root in 1 cup water for 15 minutes. Strain. Drink 1 to 2 cups a day.

Capsules: Generally, take 500 mg, 1 to 2 times daily.

Tincture: Take according to manufacturer's recommendations.

Common Name	Scientific Name	Parts Used	Therapeutic Uses
Shatavari	*Asparagus racemosus*	Roots	Tonic, premenstrual syndrome, breast milk production

Soy

BALANCE BEANS

Miso, soy sauce, tempeh, tofu—these and other foods derived from soybeans have been a cornerstone of Asian cuisine and nutrition for centuries. Soybean contains a full complement of essential amino acids, making it an important part of any vegetarian or vegan diet.

Soy is rich in phytoestrogens, plant compounds chemically similar to the hormone estrogen. Hence, herbalists suggest soy extracts to help relieve menopausal symptoms, including hot flashes and night sweats. However, because soy may increase risk of breast cancer in some women, use of extracts for menopausal symptoms remains controversial.

Soy is a member of the pea family.

▶ OBTAINING AND USING

The space it takes to grow a few soybeans in the home garden is hardly worth the effort when soybeans and soy-based products are so widely available and relatively inexpensive wherever food products are sold.

Diet: Soy foods should be part of a wholesome diet. Avoid processed soy "junk" food, and focus on edamame, soy nuts, miso, and tempeh.

Extracts: Take 50 to 90 mg a day soy isoflavones.

▶ PRECAUTIONS

Soy is healthful when consumed as part of a varied, wholesome diet. Until more research is done, breast cancer survivors should avoid combining soy extracts with tamoxifen (or should avoid therapeutic doses) because of possible plant-drug interactions.

Common Name	Scientific Name	Parts Used	Therapeutic Uses
Soy	*Glycine max*	Seeds (beans)	Hormone health, heart health, protein source

Yogurt

GO PRO(BIOTIC)!

A delicious addition to anybody's diet, yogurt is a valuable health tool as well. Yogurt is typically made by fermenting cow's milk with strains of *Lactobacillus* bacteria. Yogurts containing live bacteria ("active cultures") are considered probiotic and have health benefits for digestion and women's reproductive health. A recent study found that probiotic yogurt helped relieve constipation, diarrhea, inflammatory bowl syndrome, and lactose intolerance.

For women, yogurt's calcium content is of special interest. An estimated eight million American women have osteoporosis, a condition where bones lose mass and weaken. Eating foods high in calcium—like yogurt—can help preserve bone strength. Some yogurts are fortified with vitamin D, another key nutrient involved in keeping bones healthy.

The calcium in yogurt helps women's bones stay strong.

▶ OBTAINING AND USING

Yogurts are widely available at any grocery store. You can also make your own yogurt at home by purchasing live cultures and fermenting the milk yourself.

Selecting: Purchase yogurts that contain "live, active cultures" to take advantage of yogurt's digestive benefits. Check to see if the yogurt has been fortified with vitamin D.

Consuming: Eating one serving (1 cup) of yogurt a day has many benefits, including lowering the risk of getting a cold. Yogurt that contains *Lactobacillus reuteri* has been found to block the replication of certain illness-causing viruses. Not all brands carry that particular strain of beneficial bacteria, so look for a brand that does.

Common Name	Scientific Name	Made From	Therapeutic Uses
Yogurt	*Lactobacillus* bacteria	Fermented milk	Digestive health, bone health

DO IT YOURSELF
Hydrotherapy

Hydrotherapy is the use of water—solid, liquid, or gas—for healing purposes. You can do easy and inexpensive water therapies at home.

Have a Drink. The simplest hydrotherapy treatment is to keep your body well hydrated by drinking 48 to 64 ounces of water a day.

Rub Away Fatigue. Immediately after taking a hot bath or shower, dip a washcloth into cold water and rub the cold washcloth over one of your arms. If the cloth warms before you finish, dip in cold water again. Dry the arm thoroughly and vigorously. Repeat the same procedure on your other arm, your legs and feet, and your chest, abdomen, and buttocks.

Soak Your Feet. Hot and cold footbaths can help stimulate circulation in the feet and legs. Fill one basin with comfortably hot water and the other with cold water. Sit in a chair with the tubs side by side in front of you. Soak your feet in the hot-water tub for 60 seconds and then plunge them into the cold-water tub for 20 to 30 seconds. Repeat 3 to 4 times.

INVIGORATING FOOT SOAK

In a plastic tub large enough to accommodate your feet, add 4 drops each rosemary, eucalyptus, and peppermint essential oil. Add enough hot water (not so hot it could burn you, though) so you can submerge your feet to just below the anklebone. Soak for at least 10 minutes.

In addition to their beauty, dried herbs and flowers offer therapeutic aromas, healthful flavor for cooking, and other wellness benefits.

Appendix Therapeutic Uses

Natural remedies are amazing. Many are fabulous multitaskers and can be used to prevent and treat many different ailments. This index links natural remedies with their potential therapeutic effects. The concern is listed above the list of potential remedies. This index is not in any way intended as a therapeutic guide. Readers should consult a licensed health care professional before using any medicinal plants or remedies listed here.

Abrasions, Cuts, Sores
Calendula, p. 87
Yarrow, p. 96

Antioxidant
Bilberry, p. 42
Broccoli, p. 102
Cacao, p. 43
Gingko, p. 46
Goji, p. 78
Grapes and
grape seed, p. 47
Hibiscus, p. 49
Pomegranate, p. 105
Rosemary, p. 93
Tea, p. 40
Willow bark, p. 80

Anxiety/Nervousness
Bacopa, p. 12
Chamomile, p. 58
Hops, p. 14
Kava, p. 15
Lavender, p. 91
Lemon balm, p. 16
Motherwort, p. 120
Passionflower, p. 17
Skullcap, p. 19
Valerian, p. 20

Arthritis (osteoarthritis or rheumatoid)
Arnica, p. 70
Black cohosh, p. 116
Cat's claw, p. 72
Cayenne, p. 73
Ginger, p. 54
Stinging nettle, p. 108
Turmeric, p. 79
Willow bark, p. 80

Asthma
Eucalyptus, p. 29

Back Pain
Willow bark, p. 80

Bone Health
Spinach, p. 107
Yogurt, p. 124

Bronchitis
Butterbur, p. 27
Juniper, p. 104
Mullein, p. 33
Pelargonium, p. 34

Bruises
Arnica, p. 70
Corn silk, p. 76

Burns
Aloe, p. 84

Circulation
Ginkgo, p. 46
Horse chestnut, p. 50
Rosemary, p. 93

Cognition
Bacopa, p. 12
Ginseng, p. 10
Rosemary, p. 93

Colds, Flus
Astragalus, p. 26
Echinacea, p. 24
Elder, p. 28
Eucalyptus, p. 29
Garlic, p. 45
Ginger, p. 54
Mullein, p. 33
Pelargonium, p. 34
Sage, p. 35
Thyme, p. 36

Constipation
Psyllium, p. 65

Cough
Butterbur, p. 27
Echinacea, p. 24
Ginger, p. 54
Licorice, p. 31
Marshmallow root, p. 32
Peppermint, p. 64
Sage, p. 35
Slippery elm, p. 66
Thyme, p. 36

Dermatitis
Avocado, p. 86
Calendula, p. 87
Coconut oil, p. 88
Grindelia, p. 90
Oatmeal, p. 92

Diabetes
Aloe, p. 84
Asian ginseng, p. 10
Cinnamon, p. 44

Diarrhea
Barberry, p. 56
Chamomile, p. 58
Fennel, p. 59
Goldenseal, p. 61
Peppermint, p. 64

Diuretic
Corn silk, p. 76
Dandelion, p. 77
Hibiscus, p. 49
Parsley, p. 63

Eczema
Avocado, p. 86
Calendula, p. 87
Chamomile, p. 58
Coconut oil, p. 88
Witch hazel, p. 95

Heart Health
Cacao, p. 43
Garlic, p. 45
Grapes and
grape seed, p. 47
Hawthorn, p. 48
Hibiscus, p. 49
Pomegranate, p. 105
Psyllium, p. 65
Soy, p. 123
Tea, p. 40

High Blood Pressure
Grapes and
grape seed, p. 47
Parsley, p. 63
Yarrow, p. 96

Indigestion
Cardamom, p. 57
Chamomile, p. 58
Fennel, p. 59
Ginger, p. 54
Goldenseal, p. 61
Hops, p. 14
Lemon balm, p. 16
Peppermint, p. 64

Inflammation
Cacao, p. 43
Calendula, p. 87
Comfrey, p. 75
Ginger, p. 54
Tea, p. 40
Turmeric, p. 79
Witch hazel, p. 95
Yarrow, p. 96

Insomnia
Hops, p. 14
Lemon balm, p. 16
Passionflower, p. 17
Skullcap, p. 19
Valerian, p. 20

Menopause
Black cohosh, p. 116
Dong quai, p. 119
Hops, p. 14
Kava, p. 15
Shatavari, p. 122

Migraine Headaches
Butterbur, p. 27
Feverfew, p. 13

Premenstrual Syndrome
Black cohosh, p. 116
Chaste tree, p. 118
Dong quai, p. 119
Shatavari, p. 122

Prostate Health
Pomegranate, p. 105
Pygeum, p. 106
Saw palmetto, p. 100
Spinach, p. 107
Stinging nettle, p. 108
Tomato, p. 109

Psoriasis
Aloe, p. 84
Coconut oil, p. 88
Juniper, p. 104

Reproductive Health, Female
Dong quai, p. 119
Motherwort, p. 120
Raspberry leaf, p. 121
Soy, p. 123

Reproductive Health, Male
Broccoli, p. 102
Horny goat weed, p. 103

Sore Throat
Licorice, p. 31
Marshmallow root, p. 32
Sage, p. 35
Slippery elm, p. 66

Urinary Tract Health
Cranberry, p. 114
Juniper, p. 104
Parsley, p. 63
Uva ursi, p. 110

NATURE'S BEST REMEDIES:
THE WORLD OF HEALTH AND HEALING ALL AROUND YOU

PRODUCED BY NATIONAL GEOGRAPHIC PARTNERS, LLC
1145 17th Street NW
Washington, DC 20036-4688 USA

ISSN 2160-7141

Printed and distributed by Time Inc. Books
225 Liberty Street
New York, NY 10281

To order this or other National Geographic Collectors Editions, visit us
online at shopng.com/specialeditions.

Printed in the U.S.A.

Made in the USA
Middletown, DE
18 May 2018